AIMR Conference Proceedings
Closing the Gap between Financial Reporting and Reality

The Webcast of Baruch Lev's conference presentation "The New Value Investing" can be viewed at www.aimrdirect.org.

28–29 October 2002
Boston

Jane B. Adams
David M. Blitzer
Martin S. Fridson, CFA, *moderator*
Bruce A. Gulliver, CFA
Walter V. Haslett, CFA
Charles L. Hill, CFA

Baruch Lev
Patricia A. McConnell
Thomas R. Robinson, CFA
Donald J. Smith
David A. Zion, CFA

Association for Investment Management and Research®

Dedicated to the Highest Standards of Ethics, Education, and
Professional Practice in Investment Management and Research.

> To obtain an *AIMR Product Catalog*, contact
> AIMR, 560 Ray C. Hunt Drive, Charlottesville, Virginia 22903, U.S.A.
> Phone 434-951-5499; Fax 434-951-5262; E-mail info@aimr.org
> or
> visit AIMR's Web site at www.aimr.org
> to view the AIMR publications list.

CFA®, Chartered Financial Analyst™, AIMR-PPS®, GIPS®, and Financial Analysts Journal® are just a few of the trademarks owned by the Association for Investment Management and Research®. To view a list of the Association for Investment Management and Research's trademarks and the Guide for Use of AIMR's Marks, please visit our Web site at www.aimr.org.

©2003, Association for Investment Management and Research

All rights reserved. No part of this publication may be reproduced, stored in a retrieval system, or transmitted, in any form or by any means, electronic, mechanical, photocopying, recording, or otherwise, without prior written permission of the copyright holder.

AIMR CONFERENCE PROCEEDINGS
(USPS 013-739 ISSN 1535-0207) 2003

Is published five times a year in March, April, twice in August, and September, by the Association for Investment Management and Research at 560 Ray C. Hunt Drive, Charlottesville, VA. **Periodical postage paid at Charlottesville, Virginia, and additional mailing offices.**

This publication is designed to provide accurate and authoritative information with regard to the subject matter covered. It is sold with the understanding that the publisher is not engaged in rendering legal, accounting, or other professional services. If legal advice or other expert assistance is required, the services of a competent professional should be sought.

Copies are mailed as a benefit of membership to CFA® charterholders. Subscriptions also are available at $100.00 USA. For one year. Address all circulation communications to AIMR Conference Proceedings, 560 Ray C. Hunt Drive, Charlottesville, Virginia 22903, USA; Phone 434-951-5499; Fax 434-951-5262. For change of address. Send mailing label and new address six weeks in advance.

Postmaster: Please send address changes to AIMR Conference Proceedings, Association for Investment Management and Research, P.O. Box 3668, Charlottesville, Virginia 22903.

ISBN 0-935015-89-2
Printed in the United States of America
March 10, 2003

Editorial Staff
Kathryn Dixon Jost, CFA
Editor

Roger S. Mitchell
Book Editor

Jaynee M. Dudley
Production Manager

Sophia E. Battaglia
Assistant Editor

Rebecca L. Bowman
Assistant Editor

Kelly T. Bruton/Lois A. Carrier
Composition and Production

Contents

Authors	v
Overview: Why the Gap Opened Martin S. Fridson, CFA	1
Panel Discussion: The Measurement and Reporting of Earnings Charles L. Hill, CFA; David M. Blitzer; and Thomas R. Robinson, CFA	5
Revelations from Financial Reporting Bruce A. Gulliver, CFA	13
The Magic of Pension Accounting David A. Zion, CFA	24
Accounting (or Not) for Employee Stock Options Jane B. Adams	36
Accounting and Reporting for Derivatives and Hedging Transactions Donald J. Smith	44
Derivatives and the Enron Debacle Walter V. Haslett, CFA	54
The Current and Future State of Financial Reporting Patricia A. McConnell	60
Appendix A. Summary of SFAS No. 87	68
Appendix B. Summary of SFAS No. 123	71
Appendix C. Summary of SFAS No. 133	73
Appendix D. Summary of SFAS No. 141	75
Appendix E. Summary of SFAS No. 142	78

Selected Publications

AIMR

Benchmarks and Attribution Analysis, 2001

Best Execution and Portfolio Performance, 2001

Core-Plus Bond Management, 2001

Developments in Quantitative Investment Models, 2001

Equity Portfolio Construction, 2002

Equity Research and Valuation Techniques, 2002

Evolution in Equity Markets: Focus on Asia, 2001

Fixed-Income Management: Credit, Covenants, and Core-Plus, 2003

Fixed-Income Management for the 21st Century, 2002

Hedge Fund Management, 2002

Investment Counseling for Private Clients III, 2001

Investment Counseling for Private Clients IV, 2002

Investment Firms: Trends and Issues, 2001

Organizational Challenges for Investment Firms, 2002

Research Foundation

Anomalies and Efficient Portfolio Formation, 2002
by S.P. Kothari and Jay Shanken

The Closed-End Fund Discount, 2002
by Elroy Dimson and Carolina Minio-Paluello

Common Determinants of Liquidity and Trading, 2001
by Tarun Chordia, Richard Roll, and Avanidhar Subrahmanyam

Country, Sector, and Company Factors in Global Equity Portfolios, 2001
by Peter J.B. Hopkins and C. Hayes Miller, CFA

International Financial Contagion: Theory and Evidence in Evolution, 2002
by Roberto Rigobon

Real Options and Investment Valuation, 2002
by Don M. Chance, CFA, and Pamela P. Peterson, CFA

Risk Management, Derivatives, and Financial Analysis under SFAS No. 133, 2001
by Gary L. Gastineau, Donald J. Smith, and Rebecca Todd, CFA

The Role of Monetary Policy in Investment Management, 2000
by Gerald R. Jensen, Robert R. Johnson, CFA, and Jeffrey M. Mercer

Term-Structure Models Using Binomial Trees, 2001
by Gerald W. Buetow, Jr., CFA, and James Sochacki

Authors

We would like to thank Martin S. Fridson, CFA, for serving as moderator at this conference and for writing the overview for this proceedings. We also wish to express our sincere gratitude to the authors listed below for their contributions to both the conference and this proceedings:

Jane B. Adams is a managing director at Maverick Capital, Ltd. Previously, she served as director of accounting/tax equity research at Credit Suisse First Boston and as deputy chief accountant in the Office of the Chief Accountant at the U.S. SEC. Ms. Adams chairs AIMR's Financial Accounting Policy Committee and is a member of the International Accounting Standards Board's Share-Based Payments Advisory Group and the Financial Accounting Standards Board's User Advisory Council. She was awarded the New York State Haskins Gold Medal for receiving the highest scores on the C.P.A. examination in New York. Ms. Adams holds a B.A. from Vassar College and an M.B.A. from Pace University Graduate School of Business.

David M. Blitzer is managing director and chairman of the index committee at Standard & Poor's. Previously, he served as corporate economist at the McGraw-Hill Companies and as a senior economic analyst at National Economic Research Associates. Mr. Blitzer is the author of *Outpacing the Pros: Using Indices to Beat Wall Street's Savviest Money Managers*. He is a member of the editorial board of the *Journal of Indices* and is a regular contributor to Equity Insights and MarketScope. Mr. Blitzer holds a B.S. from Cornell University, an M.A. from George Washington University, and a Ph.D. from Columbia University.

Martin S. Fridson, CFA, is CEO of FridsonVision LLC, an investment research organization. He is the youngest person ever inducted into the Fixed Income Analysts Society Hall of Fame, and he was elected to the Institutional Investor All-America Research Team. Additionally, Mr. Fridson received the Outstanding Financial Executive Award from the Financial Management Association International. He is the author of *How to Be a Billionaire*, *It Was a Very Good Year*, and *Investment Illusions*. Mr. Fridson holds a B.A. from Harvard University and an M.B.A. from Harvard Business School.

Bruce A. Gulliver, CFA, is president and chief investment officer at Jefferson Research & Management. Previously, he taught finance in the graduate business program at American University and the undergraduate program at California State Polytechnic University. Mr. Gulliver is a member of the Portland Society of Financial Analysts and the U.S. Institute of Energy Economics. He holds a B.A. from Hastings College and an M.B.E. and a Ph.D. from Claremont Graduate School.

Walter V. Haslett, CFA, is president and chief investment officer at Write Capital Management, a derivatives-based investment management firm. Additionally, he serves as vice president and cochairman of the education committee for the Financial Analysts of Philadelphia. Mr. Haslett holds a B.S. from Shippensburg University, an M.B.A. from Drexel University, and an M.L.A. from the University of Pennsylvania.

Charles L. Hill, CFA, is director of research at Thomson Financial/First Call, where he is responsible for planning new quantitative products and maintaining the quality of existing quantitative products. He also serves as the chief financial analyst for Thomson Financial/First Call earnings data. Previously, Mr. Hill was a technology analyst at Scudder, Stevens & Clark; Kidder, Peabody, & Company; Bache (now Prudential); and Quantum Associates. He is featured regularly on radio and television newscasts and is frequently quoted in the leading financial print media. Mr. Hill holds a B.S. from the University of Delaware and an M.B.A. from Harvard University.

Patricia A. McConnell is a senior managing director at Bear, Stearns & Company, Inc., where she serves as head of the accounting and taxation group in equity research. She is a certified public accountant and chair of AIMR's Global Financial Reporting Committee and past vice chair of the International Accounting Standards Board. Ms. McConnell has been named to Institutional Investor's All-America Research Team of financial analysts for the past 12 years. She holds an M.Ph. and an M.B.A. from New York University.

Thomas R. Robinson, CFA, is associate professor of accounting at the University of Miami, where he teaches financial statement analysis. He also serves as a senior investment consultant for Earl M. Foster Associates. Previously, Mr. Robinson practiced public accounting and has served as a consultant to law firms, accounting firms, professional associations, and governmental agencies. He is a past president and current board member of the Miami Society of Financial Analysts.

Donald J. Smith is associate professor of finance and faculty director of the M.B.A. program at the Boston University School of Management. He is a member of the board of advisors of the International Association of Financial Engineers. Mr. Smith coauthored *Interest Rate and Currency Swaps: A Tutorial* and *Risk Management, Derivatives, and Financial Analysis under SFAS No. 133*. Mr. Smith holds a Ph.D. from the School of Business Administration at the University of California at Berkeley.

David A. Zion, CFA, is an accounting and tax policy analyst at Credit Suisse First Boston. Previously, he served as a senior accountant at Deloitte & Touche and was a core member of Bear, Stearns & Company's accounting group. Mr. Zion is a member of the Financial Accounting Standards Board's Financial Performance Reporting Task Force. He holds a B.S. from Binghamton University.

Overview: Why the Gap Opened

Martin S. Fridson, CFA
CEO
FridsonVision LLC
New York City

This proceedings is devoted to closing the gap between financial reporting and reality. This gap has long cried out to be closed, yet until recently, most investors took companies' reported earnings at face value. The authors in this proceedings do not.

For many years, the authors in this proceedings watched as earnings were inflated by a variety of financial reporting gimmicks, including aggressive revenue recognition, underreserving for credit losses, and a slowness to write down obsolete inventory. In general, little notice was taken of this trickery, except by a few professional short sellers and, of course, those who contributed to this book.

The press, which is meant to be the watchdog in the financial markets, could have helped by paying more attention to the reality underlying reported earnings. A few reporters and columnists did, in fact, try to alert investors to the dangers of aggressive accounting. But for the most part, the newspapers quite reasonably allocated their editorial space according to the indicated interests of their readers. Most readers appeared to be indifferent to the integrity of financial reporting, so the press never made it a major focus.

A handful of hardcore followers of financial reporting issues wished that the media would increase its coverage. But never in their wildest dreams did they expect accounting tricks to make front-page headlines day after day, as they have for much of 2002. Financial chicanery became a page-one story only after corporations took the slippery practices to an entirely new level.

The outrages that came to light in recent months went beyond merely stretching the truth to book a few extra sales in the current quarter. Companies literally manufactured profits out of nothing. These feats required exploitation of off-balance-sheet entities and mirror transactions on a previously undreamed-of scale.

A question naturally arises: Why, in a matter of just a few years, did companies drastically escalate their abuse of the financial reporting standards? Was there a spontaneous outbreak of greed among corporate managers? That is one interpretation that commentators have advanced, but it lacks credibility in my mind. My study of history suggests that, in reality, greed has been around for quite a while.

I have even heard people seriously suggest that former president Bill Clinton created the problem by setting a bad moral tone. The idea, I take it, is that after staying on the straight and narrow all their lives, impressionable CEOs adopted Clinton as their role model and strayed from the path of virtue. This hypothesis, too, somehow fails to satisfy me as a reason for the proliferation of financial reporting misdeeds. A simpler explanation is the 1990s movement toward aligning management and shareholder interests.

Old-Style vs. New-Style Manipulation

I have observed the impact of this change in the course of periodically updating my book, *Financial Statement Analysis: A Practitioner's Guide*.[1] In the period leading up to the first edition's publication in 1991, most companies were still compensating their senior management on the basis of reported earnings. Managers had an incentive to manipulate and misrepresent profits, but their gain did not depend on deceiving the market.

By way of illustration, suppose that a corporation lengthens the estimated depreciable lives of its assets for financial reporting purposes. (Tax reporting is an altogether different matter.) Depreciation expense goes down, earnings go up, and the CEO's bonus increases. In economic terms, naturally, the company is no better off than before, because the rise in reported earnings represents no change in cash flow.

Experienced investors can easily detect the liberalization of a company's accounting assumptions. The giveaway is that the ratio of depreciation expense to underdepreciated fixed assets declines. To offset this drop in earnings quality, investors will reduce the company's earnings multiple. The net result is that the stock price will remain unchanged, even though both the company's reported profits and the

---
[1] Martin S. Fridson, *Financial Statement Analysis: A Practitioner's Guide*, 3rd Edition (New York: John Wiley & Sons, 2002).

CEO's bonus rise. Senior management will achieve its compensation objective without fooling the market.

This state of affairs existed until the early 1990s. At that point, corporate America began responding to complaints that senior managers' financial success was not directly tied to their success in increasing shareholder wealth. Proponents of corporate governance reform instead argued that existing compensation plans encouraged senior managers to build empires and accumulate perks.

The reformers' proposed remedy was to link the CEO's compensation to increases in the stock price rather than to increases in stated profits. No longer would senior managers receive huge cash bonuses for jacking up reported earnings through cosmetic accounting changes. Instead, their goal would be to participate in stock price appreciation through substantial ownership of stock options.

In principle, improved alignment of management and shareholder interests is an excellent idea. There is a dark side to it, however. For a manager who is inclined to game the compensation scheme, it is no longer good enough to manipulate financial statements in ways that are transparent to investors. Under the new arrangement, the CEO must somehow convert an illusory increase in profits into a genuine rise in the stock price. Beating the system now requires financial reporting gimmicks that deceive the market.

By 2002, when the third edition of my financial statement analysis book appeared, accounting chicanery had mushroomed as an unintended consequence of the increased use of stock options in executive compensation. The 1990s represented a golden era of financial reporting hanky panky, which was great news for people who made their living by uncovering such monkey business. Unfortunately, the erosion of the reliability of companies' financial statements has produced devastating consequences for investors.

Scope of the Program

This proceedings attempts to answer several questions concerning financial reporting that are vital to practitioners:

- How can you spot companies that are playing fast and loose with the rules before they blow up and leave you with heavy losses?
- What do the accounting rules actually say about complex issues (such as pensions, intangible assets, employee stock options [ESOs], and derivatives), and how are those rules likely to change in the future?
- How can investors sort out the many conflicting versions of what earnings are?

I must emphasize that we are not talking about rounding errors. According to a recent *Wall Street Journal* report, over the latest 12 months ending 30 June 2002, the companies constituting the S&P 500 Index reported earnings of $26.74 a share. But the picture looks far different in terms of *core earnings*, as defined by Standard & Poor's. (This is one of several improved measures of corporate profitability that have been proposed. Standard & Poor's methodology emphasizes reflecting the actual cost of pension obligations and expensing ESOs.) Calculating the S&P 500 companies' performance on the basis of core earnings pushes the per-share figure down from $26.74 to $18.48, a reduction of nearly one-third.

How material are the differences among alternative earnings measures when it comes to valuation? To give you an idea, suppose you calculate the price/earnings multiple of the S&P 500 based on the latest 12-month "operating earnings" reported by the companies. This number, in effect, is management saying, "Here is the correct way to look at our earnings. It is not necessarily the way we told you to gauge our earnings last quarter. Nor is it necessarily a way that makes us comparable to other companies in our industry. Our operating earnings per share *is* the number that presents us in the best possible light." Based on these highly subjective earnings, the S&P 500's multiple is 24 times. Calculated on the basis of U.S. GAAP net income, by contrast, the multiple is 37 times. Finally, if you apply Standard & Poor's core earnings concept, the S&P 500's multiple soars to 54 times. In short, determining whether the stock market is rich or cheap, as indicated by the index's price/earnings ratio, hinges on how earnings are defined.

Earnings Definitions

By some measures, the market could still be considered quite expensive, despite the drastic drop from its peak. Vigilance on the part of analysts is therefore the watchword for the panel discussion on the measurement and reporting of earnings. Although no one knows for certain what the next accounting scandal will be, all of the panelists (Charles Hill, David Blitzer, and Thomas Robinson) agree that the investment community has not seen the last of clever earnings-inflating gimmicks. To that end, these panelists debate the perennial question of who has the most accurate earnings number and offer many insights into the games a company can play with its earnings.

Hill, for example, maintains that adjusting a company's GAAP earnings is both legitimate and desirable, despite the number of abuses that have occurred in these types of adjustments. Blitzer summarizes the significance of Standard & Poor's core earnings approach and its goal of reflecting what a company earns in its main business. Robinson makes the point that many other numbers besides earnings come into play in valuing company, a fact that often seems to be ignored. Specific questions regarding pro forma reporting, the Sarbanes–Oxley Act, option expensing, and investor confidence, among other topics, are also addressed.

Today, now that analysts have a better idea of what is in a company's earnings number and can decompose that number in terms of high- and low-quality earnings, a company's financial problems can typically be detected by a thorough examination of its financial statements. Bruce Gulliver provides copious examples in which the financial health of a company could have been detected if only analysts had not taken the numbers provided in financial statements at face value.

After learning from his own mistakes, Gulliver developed a rating system to identify potential underperformance. He maintains that this disciplined approach to financial analysis can help unearth four particularly insidious "diseases," all of which were common in the 1990s: competitive changes in either the industry or the company's competitive situation within that industry; bad acquisitions; aggressive accounting; and financial deterioration. To diagnose these diseases, analysts have to scrutinize a company's efficiency of operations, cash flow quality, earnings quality, and balance sheet quality. Gulliver shows how analysts can adjust the traditional ratios and time-series indicators to ascertain the true health of a company.

Pension Accounting

Pension accounting remains one of the most opaque areas in financial statements. Nonetheless, David Zion has managed to simplify the process. He is the bearer of both good and bad news for those investors and analysts who are earnestly trying to identify the companies that have the most exposure to defined-benefit plans and the extent to which exposure to the plan affects earnings.

Even though smoothing and quality of earnings issues can often lead investors and analysts astray, Zion identifies four types of exposure—shareholder, balance sheet, earnings, and cash flow—that can be measured and specifically evaluated. He relies on a variety of accounting and reporting adjustments to obtain an accurate representation of the economic realities of a company's pension accounting. His analysis reveals that some companies have a lot of exposure to their pension plans, but the majority of them do not.

Employee Stock Options

Even though the intricacies of pension accounting are, for the most part, penetrable, the debate over accounting for ESOs rages on because, in Jane Adams' view, the status quo accounting and reporting methods are deficient. After a brief review of the accounting methods used for measuring ESOs and the information that is provided about employee stock compensation plans in financial statements, Adams concludes that investors should actively support the accounting standard setters who are working to reform the accounting for these awards.

The corporate argument against expensing options has evolved over the years, but Adams maintains that even its latest iteration lacks substance. In the meantime, Adams suggests that analysts study a company's ESO disclosures in the notes of financial statements to unearth, for example, the number of options granted, exercised, or forfeited. In addition, she lists a number of questions that should be asked when performing comparative analyses of companies' plans.

Derivatives Market

Statement of Financial Accounting Standard (SFAS) No. 133 ranks as one of the most complex (and at more than 1,000 pages, most lengthy) accounting standards ever issued by the Financial Accounting Standards Board (FASB).[2] The new rules for derivatives accounting require that analysts have an unprecedented understanding of how derivatives work, how they are valued, and how they will perform when used as a hedge. Donald Smith describes how the rules are transforming the financial reporting landscape. He believes that because more transactions are now characterized as derivatives, the need to account for them is more important than ever before.

To illustrate the challenges posed by derivatives and why the U.S. SEC instructed the FASB to make the necessary changes to get derivatives reported on the balance sheet, Smith discusses the rationale behind and consequences of Procter & Gamble's infamous swap with Bankers Trust in the early 1990s. Then, after reviewing the sweeping changes introduced by SFAS No. 133, Smith discusses the three types of risk that now drive the accounting and reporting process for derivatives. He also defines the

---

[2]For a summary of SFAS No. 133, please see Appendix C.

characteristics of a derivative and an embedded derivative and outlines the accounting and reporting treatment of different types of hedges required under SFAS No. 133. He counsels analysts to be aware of two major implications: the new standard's redefinition of risk and the fact that the value of a financial asset or liability shown on the balance sheet is now neither the original cost nor the current market value.

As the derivatives markets grow ever more vast, they play an increasingly critical economic role for the purposes of hedging, speculation, and price discovery. As Walter Haslett warns, however, investors must thoroughly understand these markets before getting involved in them. Catastrophes can be averted if investors, managers, analysts, and traders are able to recognize the "trigger events" that can affect their transactions and are able to confirm that proper risk controls are in place.

To illustrate the problems that can be encountered with the derivatives market, Haslett discusses the Orange County investment pool debacle and the disasters that occurred at Barings Bank, Metallgesellschaft, Long-Term Capital Management, and the Enron Corporation. Each of these events, he argues, had as its genesis at least one or more of the following weaknesses: ignorance, poor risk controls, inadequate supervision, mismatches between hedged and hedging instruments, or a failure to understand the difference between hedging and speculating.

Financial Reporting Evolution

According to Patricia McConnell's overview of the current and future state of financial reporting, the recent financial debacles mirror the evolution of another boom-and-bust period at the end of the 1960s and into the 1970s. Accountants were seen as the primary villains, and the formation of the FASB led to rule-based, as opposed to principle-based, accounting standards, with more voluminous implementation guidance than anyone could have imagined.

Refusing to place blame solely on the auditing/accounting profession, however, McConnell suggests that analysts and investors are equally culpable. She also cautions that returning to a more principle-based system, as some have advocated, will not necessarily improve the situation. She points out that the current hot-button issues, such as incomplete and incomprehensible disclosures, off-balance-sheet financing, and fair value accounting, have long been on the FASB's agenda and that the quality of financial reporting is higher than it has ever been. If the investment community really wants to have an impact on the information that will be available in the future, it should turn its attention toward resolving certain emerging issues, namely, the form and content of financial statements, revenue recognition, and smoothing volatility in earnings.

Conclusion

I hope I have whetted your appetite for the material that follows and that the information provided by the authors will leave you better equipped to deal with the new world of financial reporting. It is a more exciting world than ever before and, in the minds of many investors, more exciting than it ought to be. But that is the current environment, and these authors provide fresh insights into how to make the most of it.

Panel Discussion: The Measurement and Reporting of Earnings

Charles L. Hill, CFA
Director of Research
Thomson Financial/First Call
Boston

David M. Blitzer
Managing Director and Chairman of the Index Committee
Standard & Poor's
New York City

Thomas R. Robinson, CFA
Associate Professor
University of Miami
Coral Gables, Florida

The question of what constitutes earnings can be answered in a variety of ways. This panel discussion provides differing views on what ought to constitute earnings and what analysts and investors are best advised to examine.

Hill: I would like to emphasize that I think adjusting a company's GAAP earnings is not only legitimate but also desirable. For example, if a company is earning roughly 50 cents a share each quarter and in one of those quarters realizes a gain on the sale of an asset that netted $1, should this company be valued on the $2 of annual operating earnings or the $3 that includes the asset sale? I do not think anybody would say that the asset sale should be included in earnings for valuation purposes. Unfortunately, no right answer exists. It is all in the eyes of the beholder as to what earnings components are considered nonrecurring or nonoperating.

I think the general consensus is that adjusting GAAP earnings to exclude nonrecurring and nonoperating items is proper and desirable, but the Financial Accounting Standards Board (FASB) has not issued a definition of what those adjustments should be. The FASB has not specified the "correct" adjustments because of the difficulty in overcoming the one-size-fits-all issue.

Now, having said that adjusting the numbers is legitimate and desirable, I would be the first to admit that some abuses have occurred in these types of adjustments. But similar abuses have occurred before; the instances of such abuses certainly have a cyclical nature, especially when companies find themselves in a "frothy" period. Companies start pushing the envelope, particularly once their earnings begin to slow down or the economy slows and the companies are under pressure to keep their earnings at past levels. The most recent abuses, however, were worse than in other cycles because the bubble leading up to them was bigger and longer.

Also different from prior cycles is the issue of analyst objectivity. Attention is now being called to the fact that something must be done to eliminate the conflicts between analysts and the investment banking firms for which they work. The analyst's job is to be the gatekeeper. As such, the analyst must decide the proper earnings basis to use to value the stock. Earnings can be used for a lot of things, but in most cases, earnings are being used for valuation purposes, the "E" in the P/E, so to speak.

Blitzer: I would like to give a quick summary of Standard & Poor's (S&P's) core earnings effort, where it came from, and what it tries to do.

In the last few years of this most recent bull market, accounting (among other things) became very creative. The reasons for this creativity were, in

---

Editor's Notes: Martin Fridson, CFA (the moderator of the conference), joined in the panel discussion. For more on the measurement and reporting of earnings, please see "Variations on a Theme: The Measurement and Reporting of Earnings, October 29, 2002, Remarks of Thomas R. Robinson, PhD, CPA, CFP, CFA" at www.trrassoc.com/pages/6/index.htm.

part, to sustain the bull market, to sustain the wonderful earnings that were being generated, and probably to sustain the value of at least a few of the employee stock option grants.

In response to this accounting creativity, several of us at S&P began to discuss the viability of defining "true" earnings, otherwise known as pro forma earnings, operating earnings, or core earnings. Our goal was to be able to define the earnings from a company's main or core business—that is, not what it earns from how it runs its pension plan or how it finances itself or what asset sales it had over the past couple of years but, rather, what it earns in its main business, whether it is making cars, printing newspapers, building computers, or financing other companies.

We wanted a definition that would be reasonably, if not completely, consistent from company to company and from time period to time period. One of the frustrations of using operating earnings or pro forma earnings is that even with two head-to-head competitors in the same industry, the analyst often has to adjust at least one of the two companies' financial statements before being able to compare them.

We wanted to keep our definition fairly brief; no one wants to rewrite the FASB standards. Thus, we started with net income according to GAAP because almost everyone understands that number. We then agreed on a series of adjustments for the most common nonrecurring or special items, such as those associated with employee stock options, write-offs, and pensions.

Throughout the development of this project, the lesson that was most thoroughly driven home to us was that during the bull market, all of us—analysts, investors, and portfolio managers—stopped doing our homework. That has to change; we have to do our homework. For example, if we are valuing a technology company, we better know how it is handing out options because if we do not, our income estimate (whether it is for this year, last year, or next year) will be off not by 10–20 cents but by 10–20 *percent*. Furthermore, we need to understand how the company is dealing with its pension plan, because if we do not, we will make an equally egregious error in estimating the company's income.

S&P wants to encourage analysts to take the income statement apart piece by piece to see what is in there, why it is in there, and what it means. Any step in that direction will increase the confidence investors have about the numbers they are using, and if investors feel more confident about the numbers, they may begin to feel more confident about the stock market.

Robinson: The analogy I like to use for describing analysts' and others' use of earnings is that of a pilot flying an airplane. Pilots use dozens of instruments to fly a plane, but I will talk about just four of them in the context of earnings. The airspeed indicator tells how fast the plane is going; the altitude indicator tells how high the plane is; the heading indicator tells in which compass direction the plane is traveling; and the attitude indicator tells the plane's position relative to the earth (whether the plane is pointing up or down and whether it is turning left or right). All of those instruments provide important information, but imagine if all of those instruments in the cockpit were consolidated into one instrument and it showed a reading of zero. The pilot would know the plane had a problem, but the pilot would not be sure why.

In the investment business, all of us (analysts, investors, and portfolio managers) tend to focus on a single number, and more often than not, that number is earnings. We have to take a step back and look at more than only a single number. We have to look at all the financial statements. If a company is playing games with its earnings, a very nice aspect of the double-entry accounting system is that those games can be discovered somewhere in the company's balance sheet or statement of cash flow. That is, a company cannot play games with earnings without having an impact on the financial statements other than the income statement. My favorite example of this situation happened about 10 years ago. Miniscribe Corporation was a disk drive company that was having trouble. It brought in a turnaround artist, and amazingly, in his first year there, the company's growth margins increased. At the same time, however, its accounts receivable days and its inventory days increased. The company was overstating revenues and understating costs of goods sold. If an analyst had been looking at only the earnings numbers, the analyst would have thought the company was doing very well. But by bringing the balance sheet, the cash flow statement, and the statement of stockholders' equity into the analysis, the analyst would have seen the entire picture. So, investors have to concentrate on doing their homework and on evaluating a company on many dimensions.

Think about the term "net income"; it is a net number. It results from deducting expenses from revenues. Net income results from both an aggregation process and a netting process. A good example of this netting happens with pensions. Pension expense or pension income is a composite number. It is composed of several different things—service cost, interest cost, estimated return on plan assets, and the impact of all of the various smoothing mechanisms. Likewise, to get a true picture of a company's earnings, the analyst cannot stop with the net number; the analyst has to step back and examine each of the net income components—the operating versus the investing versus the financing components.

Investors look at earnings for a variety of reasons, but one major reason is to value a company. When analysts value a company, they do not want to know what happened last year. They want to know what we can expect to happen in the future; the purpose of valuation is to estimate future earnings and future cash flows. When we look backwards, we are evaluating how a company's management has performed. So, even though an income item may be nonrecurring for purposes of valuation, it is the result of a management decision, which is important because, absent evidence to the contrary, management's past decisions are likely to be mirrored in its future decisions.

Pro forma earnings is the area in which most reporting abuses have occurred. I do not mean pro forma with regard to stock options, which is the way pro forma should be used—that is, where a company states net income as if it had expensed stock options—but pro forma with regard to arbitrarily picking and choosing which items to include or exclude. Trump Hotels and Casinos Resorts is a good example of this practice. It was actually the first company censored by the U.S. SEC in this area. Trump Hotels and Casinos presented pro forma earnings without nonrecurring expenses but with nonrecurring gains. Basically, the company removed the bad and left in the good to tell the story it wanted to tell, which is typical of much of today's recent abusive reporting.

The bottom line is that problems do exist with the calculation of GAAP net income, but if an alternative measure is used, a reconciliation based on the GAAP number is needed. A reconciliation would not have helped in the Trump Hotels case, however, because the problem appeared in both the GAAP number and the pro forma number and thus would not be discovered in a reconciliation. Interestingly, the SEC has been mandated by the Sarbanes–Oxley Act of 2002 (Sarbanes–Oxley) to introduce a new rule that will require a reconciliation not only of pro forma earnings but also of any other pro forma numbers to the GAAP numbers.[1] In addition, if a company omits certain information that would make that calculation material, the company will be in violation of the Securities Act of 1934. So, going forward, a company will have to be more careful about what it chooses to include and exclude for reporting purposes and how it reconciles those items.

Fridson: I would like to amplify the point about the use of the term "pro forma," the meaning of which has changed over time. When I was in business school, which was a long time ago, pro forma did not mean what it means now. Then, the pro forma concept was used in the context of mergers and investments. It involved a genuinely useful adjustment to help analysts project future earnings by estimating what recent earnings would have been if not for the radical change in the company's composition. Now, the term "pro forma" is applied to indicate that the company is providing only a subjective, non-GAAP version of its earnings. The contemporary concept of pro forma reporting has no legitimate analytical rationale; as far as I can tell, it has nevertheless been accepted without much debate.

Hill: Pro forma reporting started with the Internet companies and then spread to the other technology companies. So, it started in situations in which a company had high-value and short-life goodwill. A company would acquire (with its extremely overvalued stock) another company that was equally extremely overvalued. But because the transaction did not qualify for pooling-of-interests treatment, the new company would have had a huge amount of goodwill relative to the value of the two companies. In addition, the new company could not use the normal 40-year period to amortize the newly created goodwill but would have to use a 3- to 5-year period. So, the companies had this high-value, short-life goodwill that was severely distorting the earnings (or lack thereof) of these companies. Thus, analysts began to exclude amortization expense, which was later vindicated by the provisions of the FASB's Statement of Financial Accounting Standards (SFAS) No. 141 (*Business Combinations*) and SFAS No. 142 (*Goodwill and Other Intangible Assets*).[2] All would have been fine and good if the adjustments for nonrecurring items had stopped there, but once the door was open, companies started trying to figure out what other nonrecurring items they could shove in the adjustment. And that is where the term "pro forma" originated.

The pro forma abuse is a different kind of abuse from what we have had in the past. I would have thought that once there no longer was any goodwill amortization to exclude, this other recurring junk would be in the spotlight by itself and the exclusion of these other items would die out. And once the recent accounting and reporting scandals hit,

---

[1] The Sarbanes–Oxley Act can be found at http://news.findlaw.com/hdocs/docs/gwbush/sarbanesoxley072302.pdf. A summary can be found at www.aicpa.org/info/sarbanes_oxley_summary.htm and www.aba.com/NR/rdonlyres/000060d7ssqyrkcquadpudzc/Sarbanes-Oxley+Act+of+2002+072509999999 92.pdf.

[2] For summaries of SFAS Nos. 141 and 142, please see Appendixes D and E.

including the Enron Corporation and Worldcom debacles, I thought pro forma reporting would die out even faster because companies would want to do the right thing, but by and large, that has not happened. Some companies are taking that step. Yahoo! was one of the first companies to say no more pro forma, but the majority of the companies still have not stopped the practice, which is an unfortunate situation.

Question and Answer Session

Question: When do you anticipate that S&P will begin reporting current and historical core earnings and distribute them through Compustat?

Blitzer: Our Web sites, www.standardandpoors.com and www.coreearnings.standardandpoors.com, have background information, research papers, and some data on S&P's core earnings for the S&P 500. Presently, Compustat's Research Insight offers data on the S&P Super Composite 1500 companies beginning in 2001. By the end of the first quarter 2003, we should have history for the S&P Super Composite 1500 beginning in 1996 and current data for about another 1,500 companies outside the index. By the end of third quarter 2003, we will have data from 2001 forward for all 7,000 companies in Compustat. The history for the non-S&P Super Composite 1500 companies will be added during the second half of 2003 and into early 2004. All the history goes back to 1996, the first year when the FASB required option expenses to be reported.

Question: Will First Call's services provide a reconciliation between your operating earnings number and the GAAP number?

Hill: They already do. Unfortunately, most people don't seem to read the footnotes in First Call or in annual reports, but a reconciliation is already provided. There is a footnote trail in First Call between the operating number and the GAAP number.

The reconciliation, however, is not always in the earnings release. And until Sarbanes–Oxley was implemented, the reconciliation requirement has been only for the 10-K and the 10-Q. Little attention has been paid to putting the reconciliation in the earnings release. Until December 2001, the only limitation placed on the earnings release was that it could not be misleading. But after December 2001, the earnings release has to have a reconciliation to the GAAP number.

In a few instances, companies were providing a reconciliation in the release, but the trail between the GAAP and the adjusted number was incomplete and not always easy to follow. The SEC's intent was that an explicit trail would be given for each reconciling item. Unfortunately, the SEC's intent was not spelled out, and we tried to point out this deficiency to the SEC in the beginning. So, a company would report that it earned, say, 50 cents a share based on GAAP and 60 cents a share pro forma because of an asset-sale gain, a restructuring charge, and an inventory write-down that netted out to 10 cents. The problem was that perhaps two of those items should be excluded and one included, but the company didn't give you the information needed to make the correct adjustment. Whatever is excluded in the First Call operating number will be footnoted.

Robinson: I want to comment on Sarbanes–Oxley. It actually goes quite a bit further than the SEC has gone in the past. Sarbanes–Oxley required the SEC to put forth a new rule regarding the public disclosure of pro forma information (not only in the 10-K and in press releases), which will mandate a reconciliation and disclosure of all material facts.[3]

Hill: But the initial SEC proposals in implementing Sarbanes–Oxley still do not require a company to provide the after-tax impact of each adjusting item. The SEC doesn't require that each item be justified, and it doesn't require disclosure about items that analysts normally exclude from GAAP but that companies tend to include. For example, I have seen an asset-sale gain included in GAAP earnings and no discussion of it was made by the company, even though that item traditionally would have been excluded from GAAP earnings.

Robinson: That is correct. A company can still do that, but Sarbanes–Oxley makes it a violation of the Securities Act of 1934 if the company doesn't disclose that information when it is material information. I think companies will pay attention because penalties under the 1934 Act have been increased to up to 20 years and a $25 million fine.

Blitzer: A lot of our ability to check the prevalence of accounting abuse is going to depend, whether we like it or not, on the SEC. I think that the Sarbanes–Oxley Act has moved us a lot farther than we were before July 2002 and probably a lot farther than some of us thought we could get. But we are not home free yet; vigilance is required on the part of users of accounting data and the alleged beneficiaries of the legislation to make a little noise at times in order to encourage the SEC to enforce Sarbanes–Oxley. Otherwise, the reform may be for naught.

---

[3]The final SEC rule mandated by Sarbanes–Oxley was finalized 22 January 2003. The rule can be found at www.sec.gov/rules/final/33-8176.htm.

Fridson: The requirement to reconcile earnings announcements and formal reporting—in effect, to regulate what goes into the earnings releases—represents quite a dramatic change. Formerly, the number that the investor relations department provided to the media often diverged sharply from the GAAP earnings that later appeared in the 10-Q. Many analysts began to suspect that companies had a conscious strategy of disseminating an unduly rosy version of earnings for public consumption, perhaps in the hope that by the time the 10-Q became available analysts would be on to the next company. If that was the plan, it probably succeeded in a number of cases. So, the requirement to reconcile is a significant departure from the system that has operated in the past.

Question: Does the passion with which proponents of option expensing make their arguments put too much emphasis on net income?

Blitzer: No. A company needs to disclose any material item, and I think most of us would agree that the true cost of employee stock options is material.

The important point, as was mentioned earlier, is to look at stock option expense and its impact on earnings for both valuation and risk assessments of companies. Although S&P's analysts in the ratings division (which is separate from my division) may use core earnings, their primary concern is cash flow—whether the money will be there to pay the interest on a company's bonds when the payment date rolls around. They are concerned with whether funds used to buy back stock and limit dilution reduce funds available for other uses, including interest payments. When we compare what they do with what we do, it turns out that we have many of the same concerns.

So, focusing on the true cost of options or recognizing any other item that affects earnings is not putting too much emphasis on the income statement. Maybe the counter question is: Is the way in which most equity analysis is currently done putting too much emphasis on only earnings (and, therefore, only the P/E)? Because P/E certainly does not tell the complete story; myriad other issues affect the value of a company's stock in the present and in the future.

Hill: I think what to include and what to exclude should be left up to the investment community. I happen to think that options should be expensed, but I disagree with the idea that there is only one way to account for that transaction. We should let the investment community decide the proper accounting treatment. So, we need to ensure that investment professionals have the tools to make their own decisions. The current footnote requirement is not satisfactory. I think it would be a step forward to show options expense on a quarterly basis as part of the income statement.

Robinson: The impact of stock options goes well beyond income. For instance, there is a cash flow impact. The example I like to use is Dell Computer Corporation. If you look at Dell's financial statements over the past two years, you can see that the company reported operating cash inflows of about $1 billion per year from the tax benefits of their employee stock option plans. That cash flow now will disappear because Dell's stock price isn't rising. At the same time, Dell has been spending about $3 billion a year to buy back stock to manage the dilution that would otherwise be caused by the issuance of the stock options; that is, it wants to keep the number of shares of its outstanding stock the same. So, here is a case with a big cash outflow impact in which the large operating cash outflow is noticed but the even larger financing cash outflow is not noticed. This large financing cash outflow far exceeds the footnote disclosures that Dell made about the income effect of its options.

Also, think about options issuance in terms of the balance sheet. A lot of analysts calculate a diluted EPS number, but how many adjust book value per share for outstanding stock options? Accounting for the issuance of stock options has a lot of implications beyond net income.

Question: Do you think the recent negative news about financial reporting issues is having a material impact on the willingness of investors to participate in the market, given that they've already lost a lot of money?

Hill: The biggest problem with getting investors back into the market is that they have lost a lot of money, and that experience is going to have a prolonged impact on whether they enter the market again or not.

But the accounting-abuse scandals also have had an impact on the willingness of investors to participate in the market. Most individual investors understand that they don't have the same expertise as professionals, but as long as they feel that the playing field is reasonably level, they are willing to take their chances and accept the knocks that may follow.

Now, individual investors have a tremendous sense that they have been had and that the financial reporting system is flawed. The industry really needs to work to change these perceptions. Some of these perceptions are valid, but many are exaggerated. These perceptions are important not only in getting the individual investor back into the market but also in getting the general public to support the capitalist system. The ship is half sunk, and we had better do something to right it before we lose public support.

Robinson: I agree that we do have to get investor confidence back. Individual investors are making decisions based on P/E, and they've come to realize they can't trust the "E" in P/E. We all need to do our homework, but a lot of people weren't doing their homework in the bull market. Management wasn't doing its homework; auditors weren't doing their homework; and many analysts weren't doing their homework. We all need to start doing our homework in order to get investor confidence back and get individual investors to return to the market.

Blitzer: Yes, getting investors to trust financial reporting again is a necessary condition to restoring faith in the stock market. It is not the whole battle, but it is part of it. Restoring faith also involves restoring investors' faith in the auditors. If the auditors can't explain what they found, do I assume they didn't find anything that was really worth explaining or do I assume they can't explain it and thus maybe I should worry? It used to be that we trusted the auditors to know what to leave out; after Enron, one wonders.

Hill: Wall Street bears some responsibility in encouraging the "new-era" mantra of "this cycle is different." But the business cycle hasn't been repealed. There was too much hoopla from strategists, economists, and even Mr. Greenspan about this new-era stuff. I think we need, and needed, to pay more attention to history.

Fridson: Yes, the new-era concept is anything but new. From my informal study of history, I had long been aware that the phrase had been applied to the prosperity experienced during the Coolidge administration (1923–1929). But in the course of researching a book on historical stock market performance, I learned that the idea was old hat even in the 1920s. I found mention of a new era that referred to bullish stock market scenarios promoted way back in 1901. So, I echo the sentiment that when you start looking at history, you find that there's nothing novel about the excitement associated with a "new paradigm" or a "new era."

Hill: Just before the 1980 recession, Benjamin M. Rosen, who was at the time a sell-side electronics analyst (and who later became CEO of Compaq Computer Corporation), was speaking to the CEOs and CFOs of a number of companies in Silicon Valley. Before he began speaking, he read an article to the audience that exhorted how it was going to be different this time around because of the many new technological applications (including computers) that were emerging for the automobile, consumer products, and telecommunications industries. It was the same message we heard in the 1990s, except that in the 1990s the Internet had become part of the argument.

Rosen read from the article about how the development of a new era was a result of improved productivity, that consumers would continue to spend, and that the cyclical downturns we had experienced in the past were over. I looked around the room and everyone was nodding and smiling at each other. When Rosen finished he said, "The date of this article is June 1973, just before the last economic downturn."

Question: Are the U.S. equity markets fairly valued today?

Hill: Maybe the better question is: Why was the market so out of kilter in the 1990s? P/Es, even adjusted for interest rates, were at record levels. Records are made to be broken, but you have to be suspicious when you see valuation peaks that are 40 percent above the previous peaks, as happened in 1999 and 2000. If we had broken the record by 5 or 10 percent, I would have said, "Hallelujah, we set a new record." But when the new record is that extreme, it is telling us that stocks are overvalued.

Blitzer: Even reasonable-to-good growth for both the economy and earnings over the next two or three years still doesn't mean a quick reversion to net income of more than $50 a share, as occurred in 2000 for the S&P 500. Recovery will take four or five years. And if you accept the notion that investors are again willing to accept risk after having gone through the past 2½ years, then I think there is an opportunity for the market to make some modest gains.

The last five years of the 1990s were almost the best five years of the 20th century. The other very strong five-year period in the 20th century started, I believe, in June 1932, at which point the market was down roughly twice as far in percentage terms as it was at the most recent lows. So, if investors are willing to accept some risk, they can expect the market to go up, but they should not expect it to go up the way it did in the 1990s.

Question: Given the increased scrutiny on pensions, options, and nonrecurring items, how do you think companies will pump up earnings in the future?

Robinson: Where will the next accounting scandal be? Let's assume that we've closed the loophole on special purpose entities, that we now know what to look for in depreciation and pension expenses, and that the FASB has made changes in the way extraordinary/nonrecurring items are reported to bring some of these items back to the top of the income statement. In particular, beginning in 2003, gains and losses and early extinguishment of debt will no longer be extraordinary items. Nevertheless, some corporate managements will be creative in finding other ways to manage financial statement reporting.

Accounting abuse boils down to several standard techniques, such as capitalizing expenses instead of expensing them. For example, about 10 years ago, Cineplex Odeon was lengthening the amortization period for capitalized expenses. This was occurring during Garth Drabinsky's tenure as chairman of Cineplex Odeon, and when he was asked to leave because of the accounting games he was playing, he founded Livent. And guess what? He did it again. So, some management will continue to use the methods they have used in the past to improve earnings.

Blitzer: I think managements will continue to be creative in finding new ways to report better earnings and will continue to use the old tricks as well.

Hill: In the future, the accounting manipulations will have a different twist, but it will still be the same game. The off-balance-sheet accounting treatment that we have recently seen is not new. Back in the 1970s, Memorex Products was a hot company, selling at more than 100 times earnings. It had off-balance-sheet lease subsidiaries and very complex deals, just as Enron did. I remember when Larry Spitters, the CEO of Memorex, gave a presentation to the Boston financial community and was trying to explain how the money flowed between subsidiaries. He was in the middle of his presentation, and the audience was asking questions because it was so confusing. Finally, he threw up his hands and said, "I can't explain it."

So, when Ken Lay said he couldn't explain the $1.5 billion write-down that Enron took, it was déjà vu. We'd heard it before. These kinds of excesses occur in every cycle.

Fridson: Without question, variations on the same theme keep recurring. At the same time, I marvel at the ingenuity of managements in devising new variations. One new wrinkle that really impressed me in this cycle was the creation of an ostensibly independent entity to conduct research. This entity could book the research costs as revenue. The main company then acquired the research unit for a premium to its tangible asset value, attributing a substantial portion of the purchase price to the value created by the research. Under the conventional approach of conducting research within a consolidated subsidiary, the R&D outlays would be permanently expensed away. By conducting the same research within an allegedly independent entity, the company could ultimately transform the expenditures into an asset on its balance sheet. From the main company's standpoint, it was a clever way to get around the GAAP prohibition on capitalizing R&D expenditures. Once you look at the transaction from this angle, you recognize an obvious loophole that you figure would have been exploited years ago. But until some original thinker came up with the gambit, investors were unprepared to deal with it. Fortunately for people who make their living by exposing earnings-inflating gimmicks, managements seem to have an inexhaustible reserve of creativity.

Hill: We have a cultural problem. In our society, if a lawyer can find a way to circumvent the system, people think such behavior is acceptable not only legally but also morally. People are no longer concerned about the spirit or intent of the rules; the question they now ask themselves is: Are we violating the letter of the law? I don't know how we can change that attitude.

Question: How can we judge the legitimacy of extraordinary charges and nonrecurring events on core earnings?

Hill: This is another misuse of the word "extraordinary," and we keep stressing this point. Only a few specific items, such as the cumulative effect of an accounting change or early debt retirement, qualify as extraordinary under GAAP rules. Unfortunately, items in many footnotes referring to unusual items often are mistakenly referred to as extraordinary.

Fridson: Even in security analysts' reports a clear differentiation is not always made.

Blitzer: We debated this issue and decided we needed to dig into the data, which unfortunately, despite the SEC, are not so deeply detailed. For example, we chose to dig into the data about reversals. One gimmick is to take a huge write-off in the current year. The theory is that if a company takes a $10 million, $15 million, or $20 million hit to earnings, the stock will be affected negatively by the same amount. But when the company discovers serendipitously the following year that the write-off should have been only $7 million, the adjustment to correct that excessive write-off rolls back into income, giving the impression of a fantastic turnaround. But most of the turnaround was a figment of the company's imagination.

We looked at the accounting reversals in the Compustat data. For almost every reversal that occurred, there was a write-off the year before. It takes a little digging, but you can find out what's really happening at a company. Because even with a rule book as long as your arm, some crafty lawyer or accountant would find a way around it.

Hill: Of course, you still have the risk that a business like W.R. Grace & Company doesn't tell you about its reversals, but at least the SEC discovered what was going on and made a "poster child" of them.

Blitzer: The bottom line is that you need to do a little digging to find out whether those nonrecurring items are really nonrecurring. The presumption (being conservative) should be that if it is a loss or an expense, it is going to continue, and if it is a gain or income, it is not.

Revelations from Financial Reporting

Bruce A. Gulliver, CFA
President and Chief Investment Officer
Jefferson Research & Management
Portland, Oregon

> A company's financial problems can typically be detected by a thorough examination of its financial statements. Most problems are caused by four "diseases": changes in competitive situation, bad acquisitions, aggressive accounting stances, and general financial deterioration. These problems are reflected in the diagnostics of investment quality, cash flow quality, earnings quality, and balance sheet quality. Although detecting these problems is not easy, various techniques and resources exist to help portfolio managers and analysts uncover them.

Most analysts—equity and debt—have been humbled recently by market and corporate events. Unfortunately, the financial analysis techniques that I will describe in my presentation cannot detect every instance of corporate fraud that might exist. Nonetheless, for those who know where (and how) to look, information in the basic financial statements can reveal a number of company problems.

First, I will share with you three of the mistakes that I have made in the past and what I learned from these mistakes. Next, I will briefly describe the elements of problem identification that I used in creating the research techniques that we use at Jefferson Research & Management. I will then discuss the four corporate financial "diseases" and the "symptoms" of these diseases. Finally, I will explain several examples of how to find these problems using the "diagnostics" we have developed for ourselves and our clients as a tool for uncovering the true story presented in a company's financial statements.

The examples I highlight in my presentation do not imply fraud or any illegal activity on the part of the companies involved; they are simply illustrations of the points that I am making and are drawn from my own work. Other analysts have their own equally interesting examples from other companies.

The author would like to thank the following for their assistance in the preparation of this presentation: Jim Delisle, CFA; Jim Carlson, CMA; Laurie Wesley, CPA; and Jessica Marrash.

Learning from Prior Mistakes

The first (and biggest) mistake I made was not working with all three financial statements in depth. The income statement was my primary resource, and I made only cursory examination of both the cash flow statement and the balance sheet. Occasionally, this practice resulted in a high ranking for companies that showed high earnings growth even though their balance sheets were deteriorating.

My second mistake was to believe that the basic ratios (such as P/E, price to sales, and price to cash flow) based on "as reported" data were reliable indicators of a company's health. I have found the easily accessible cash flow from operations (CFFO), reported earnings per share (EPS), and bond ratings to be unreliable.

Under U.S. GAAP, companies are given great latitude in how they report CFFO and EPS. Some of the prescribed ways of reporting do not truly reflect how much cash flow or earnings are generated from the company's "real" business. Likewise, bond ratings are well known for lagging the realities of a company's financial situation and are seldom helpful in determining equity risk.

A third mistake that I made was to fall in love with a stock. In a world of matchmakers—Wall Street analysts, public relations firms, and media stock experts—I (along with perhaps other analysts) found myself emotionally committed to a stock long after I should have removed it from my portfolio. Comptronix Corporation is an example of my misguided loyalty to a stock in my portfolio whose income statement told partial truths. In the late 1980s, Comptronix overstated its revenues by boosting inventories and then later converted these inventories into fixed assets in a way that never hit the income statement. A complete examination of the balance sheet and cash flow statement would have raised questions about the income statement. I remember the Comptronix blow-up vividly. It occurred while I was traveling from the West Coast to the East Coast on the day before Thanksgiving. In the time it took me to make that trip, the stock fell about 70 percent after the first news of potential financial irregularities was reported.

Developing Our Rating System

In 1997, I began conducting research with the goal of developing a rating system that would identify the causes of a stock's potential underperformance. This is the system we now use at Jefferson Research & Management. I looked at many sources of information, such as U.S. SEC fraud cases, books,[1] academic studies, and of course, the CFA candidate curriculum. From among the more than 20 SEC fraud cases I studied, which I highly recommend to those who have a serious interest in financial statement analysis, two of these cases stand out.

Livent was a company in the entertainment production business. It hid advertising costs in the capitalized expenses of new theater openings. For example, when the company advertised a new play in New York, it would record the New York marketing expenses as a capitalized cost associated with the opening of a new theater in Chicago.

My personal SEC fraud favorite is the Sensormatic Electronics Corporation "clock-stopping" case. Any sports fan can appreciate the advantage of stopping the clock near the end of the game when your team is trailing. This company literally stopped the clock at the end of the quarter and kept it running until it could record the desired additional revenues in that quarter.

Interestingly, academic studies of earnings quality are found mostly in the accounting journals, not in the traditional finance journals and typically not in the journals that a CFA charterholder is likely to read. Salient articles that I found beneficial include Richard G. Sloan's seminal 1996 piece, P.M. DeChow's 1994

article, M.D. Beneish's 1997 study, and Kathryn Schipper's 1989 commentary.

The CFA candidate curriculum also provided some foundation for our development of a company financial rating system. In addition to the normal ratio analysis taught in the CFA program, I drew on the DuPont analysis—now more than 60 years old—and on the work of Ben Graham on balance sheets and cash flow. Edward Altman's Z-score—the bankruptcy predictor that was first published in 1961—also provided some insights on balance sheet items.

Four Diseases of Corporate Performance

Based on my research, I identified four diseases that can debilitate companies and their stock prices. Importantly, we have found that these diseases do not necessarily occur independently of each other.

The first disease is a competitive change either in the industry at large or in a particular company's competitive situation within that industry. For industries, such change occurs because of economic cycles and changed industry competitive factors (for example, when Japanese automakers entered the U.S. automobile market). For companies, such change can occur as a result of a transition in the company's product cycle, the introduction of new technology, or a shift in the company's competitive position within the industry. For example, a competitor may introduce a lower-cost product with better features.

The second disease involves bad acquisitions. A bad acquisition happens when a company's management assures an eventual deterioration in the company's performance (and eventually the stock price) by paying too much for an acquired company. Bad acquisitions became an epidemic by the end of the 1990s. Some of these acquisitions were initially described as being "earnings accretive," but later, when they obviously were not earnings accretive, they were described as being "revenue accretive." Finally, by the year 2000, when the prior justifications no longer could be applied to support the prices paid, these acquisitions were more often called "strategic initiatives."

The third disease is aggressive accounting. Although this disease is headline news today, it was not uncommon in the 1990s. The most noteworthy difference between then and now is that aggressive accounting, and especially fraud, recently has been practiced by much larger companies than in the past. In the past, the SEC typically investigated 15–20 fraud cases every year, but the problems at Enron Corporation and WorldCom involved unusually large, widely held companies. Enron's case (with its

---

[1] Thornton L. O'Glove, *Earnings Quality* (New York: Free Press, 1987); Howard Schilit, *Financial Shenanigans: How to Detect Accounting Gimmicks & Fraud in Financial Reports*, 2nd ed. (New York: The McGraw-Hill Companies, 2002); and Kathryn Staley, *The Art of Short Selling* (New York: John Wiley & Sons, Inc., 1997).

myriad hidden entities that generated both earnings and cash flow in mysterious ways) was quite different from the typical cases that the SEC reviews.

Finally, the fourth disease is financial deterioration, which can easily be hidden behind the appearance of a very strong income statement if analysts fail to critically examine the underlying cash flow statement and balance sheet.

Diagnosing the Diseases

To identify these four diseases, we look at four diagnostics: efficiency of operations (or investment quality), cash flow quality, earnings quality, and balance sheet quality. Each of these diagnostics can identify the symptoms of one or more of the four diseases and help focus our analytical efforts to increase our understanding of how they can affect a company and its stock price.

Efficiency of Operations. Three types of information extractable from the financial statements are worth evaluating to determine how efficient a company is in its operations. The first category is turnover, or how productively a company uses its various assets. These assets can range from inventory to receivables to plant and equipment—any asset the analyst finds helpful in ascertaining the efficiency of a business.

The second efficiency category concerns the ratios used to measure the various operating margins. Each margin can tell a different story or a different part of the story about a company's potential diseases. For example, the gross margin speaks eloquently of the company's competitive position, whereas the net margin indicates management's discipline in managing costs and a company's tax position. Another margin indicator is SG&A (sales, general, and administration) as a percentage of sales, which tells how much of a company's revenue is devoted to overhead costs.

The third category of efficiency indicators is return on capital, or how much profit a company makes on the capital that it has invested in its business. Such measures include return on investment, return on assets, and cash flow return.

These categories are all measures of the efficiency of operations. Noting that these efficiencies are managed as a way to improve the "yield" of a business, we sometimes call them investment quality measures.

Cash Flow Quality. Cash flow is often described as the ultimate litmus test of a business. Analysts often focus on CFFO, which can be deceptive. The key to identifying cash flow quality lies in isolating the cash generated from a company's business activities from the extraordinary and discontinued items that are distinct from the company's ongoing business. The fairly broad definition under GAAP of what can be included in CFFO makes this identification more important.

A good example of the need to adjust CFFO to find true cash flow is found in the financial statements of Corporate Executive Board. Over the period from third quarter 1999 to second quarter 2002, nearly 35 percent of Corporate Executive Board's CFFO was attributable to the tax benefit gained by expensing the issuance of stock options on the company's tax return. Companies are not presently required to expense newly issued stock options on their income statements, but the issuance can generate a tax credit, which occurred for many other companies as well. This tax credit is reported as a CFFO item under GAAP.

This treatment tends to overstate the cash generated from a company's business and is true of most companies with significant stock option programs. We contend that an appropriate measure of cash flow return would separate these transient events from the ongoing core cash flow a company can generate. The downward adjustment to Corporate Executive Board's CFFO in the fourth quarters of 1999, 2000, and 2001, as shown in **Figure 1**, largely reflects the elimination of this tax benefit as a source of CFFO. This adjustment to arrive at an alternative measure of cash flow may or may not change the investment decision, but it is information that should be considered.

Earnings Quality. To ascertain a company's earnings quality, an analyst needs to look at several elements affecting reported earnings, including

Figure 1. Cash Flow Quality Example: Corporate Executive Board, Third Quarter 1999– Second Quarter 2002

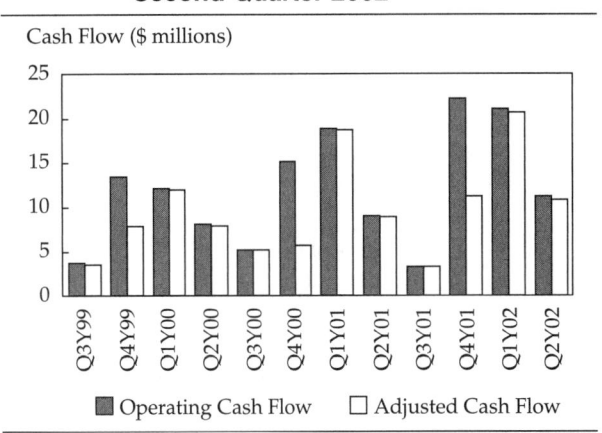

(1) the accrual rate, which is the change in the current asset section of the balance sheet compared with the sales growth rate; (2) one-time items, which can positively boost current reported earnings; (3) pension plan gains, which may inflate current earnings; (4) supporting cash flow, the measure of the amount of cash flow actually underpinning the earnings; and (5) the tax rate, particularly if the reductions have contributed to higher earnings but may not be sustainable in the long term.

Balance Sheet Quality. A company's balance sheet quality is primarily a function of its liquidity, a company's ability to meet its obligations, and its inventory and accounts receivable levels. Inventory and accounts receivable compared with sales and cost of goods sold on a day-sales-outstanding (DSO) basis can give the analyst a better understanding of how a company uses its balance sheet. This analysis is important because an increase in sales is typically associated with higher levels of inventory and accounts receivable and thus may not immediately generate cash. This analysis can also provide an indication of a lack of interest in a company's products by consumers.

Next on the balance sheet are the other accrual items, such as prepaid or deferred charges, tax valuation accounts, and prepaid taxes. These can mask or elucidate underlying changes occurring at a company. An analysis of these accounts can highlight the degree to which income is not simultaneous with cash inflow.

The symptoms of two financial problems, those arising from changes in competitive conditions and those from aggressive accounting, often show up first on the balance sheet because of GAAP's double-entry bookkeeping system. Each dollar of earnings can be attributed to either cash flow or a balance sheet item. For this reason, Enron had to go to elaborate lengths to disguise its financial deterioration. Thus, the interplay of the balance sheet with the earnings statement is essential in discovering the sustainability of earnings and potentially the survival of a company itself.

Uncovering Financial Problems

The problems that the market is dealing with today can be attributed to two predominant corporate financial diseases—changes in competitive positions and aggressive accounting practices. The "bubble" conditions of strong growth and capital flows that supported these diseases burst a while ago, but a number of companies tried to disguise this in their financial reports; Enron and Worldcom are the best-known examples of these types of deceptive practices.

Changes in Competitive Position. Lucent Technologies and Cisco Systems are two high-profile companies whose problems resulted from both industry- and company-specific competitive issues. Their stories exemplify how an observant analyst could have noticed the symptoms that would have revealed the underlying problem. All of these symptoms existed in advance, sometimes significantly in advance, of the drop in each company's stock price.

■ *Lucent.* Lucent is an example of a company operating in a sector that fell on the worst of times after enjoying the best of times. The equipment sector of the telecommunications industry had been financed heavily by extensive new investment through huge infusions of capital and was growing at an unsustainable rate. Lucent was carried along with the rest of the sector on the path to financial demise. This downward path for Lucent was evident in its financial statements, if an analyst knew where to look.

As shown in **Table 1,** by 1999, deterioration in earnings quality and investment quality had appeared as symptoms of the problems soon to overtake Lucent. Deterioration in cash flow quality followed in 2000.

One of the components of investment quality, gross margins, had fallen from approximately 55

Table 1. Lucent: Torpedo Alert Indicators, Fourth Quarter 1998–Third Quarter 2000

Indicators	1998 Q4	1999 Q1	Q2	Q3	Q4	2000 Q1	Q2	Q3
Earnings quality	W	SA	A	W	SA	SA	SA	A
Investment quality	W	SA	SA	SA	SA	SA	SA	A
Cash flow quality	SA	W	W	A	W	A	SA	SA
Valuation	W	W	W	NA	NA	NA	NA	NA
Balance sheet quality	W	A	A	W	W	W	W	W

Note: NA = no alert; W = warning; A = alert; and SA = strong alert.

percent to 45 percent even before the company hit its peak stock price in fiscal fourth quarter 1999. This was a sure indication that Lucent was facing higher costs with less ability to dictate higher prices to its customers. Return on invested capital (ROIC), a component of investment quality, started to decline later than the gross margins but fell by about half (from more than 20 percent to roughly 10 percent) in the one-year period from 1999 to 2000.

Neither cash flow quality nor cash flow generation was strong in 1999 and 2000. As **Figure 2** illustrates, beginning in the first quarter of 2000, the inconsistency in cash flow quality (the difference between reported cash flow and adjusted cash flow) was apparent. By the third quarter of 2000, CFFO was very negative, having swiftly deteriorated from a peak in the first quarter of 2000.

Figure 2. Lucent: Cash Flow Quality, First Quarter 1999–Third Quarter 2000

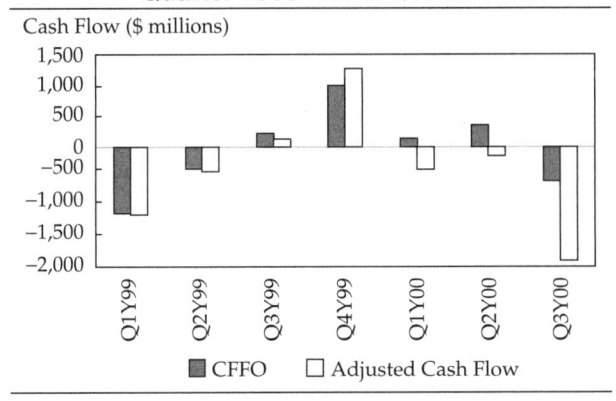

Likewise, in 1999 and 2000, Lucent's earnings quality was poor. Of its $4.8 billion of reported net income in 1999, nearly one-third, or $1.3 billion, was attributable to the cumulative effect of a pension plan accounting change. For analysts who were keeping a keen eye on earnings quality, Lucent's financial problems were identifiable. While its stock price was moving to all-time highs, its basic measures of health were declining.

■ *Cisco.* Even Cisco, a growth "darling," could not avoid the downturn in industry conditions and resulting competitive pressures in the technology industry. As shown in **Table 2,** the first symptom that financial disease existed at Cisco was a cash flow quality problem that surfaced in the third quarter of 1999. In the fourth quarter of 2000, the additional symptoms of poor investment quality and balance sheet quality were noticeable.

Cash flow quality was always an issue for Cisco in the nearly two-year period between the second quarter of 1999 and the first quarter of 2001, but it significantly worsened in the fourth quarter of fiscal 2000. As with Lucent, a large part of the difference between CFFO and actual cash flow was the tax benefit associated with the issuance of stock options. The company was less able to generate cash from its business and more reliant on its stock option plan.

During 1999, Cisco's ROIC, an indicator of investment quality, hovered around 20 percent but gradually fell to less than 15 percent by the first quarter of 2001. And Cisco's inventories on a DSO basis doubled over the four-quarter period ending with the first quarter of 2001. Historically, inventory levels had been running at less than 60 days; suddenly, they increased to about 100 days. This development, reported on Cisco's balance sheet, was an obvious deterioration in balance sheet quality that the astute analyst would have noted.

Aggressive Accounting. A range of reporting stances could be described as aggressive, but many of these aggressive accounting practices are acceptable under GAAP and become fraudulent only when company management pushes them to the extreme. We look for the following aggressive accounting practices:
- booking revenues early or without actually earning them;
- failing to record normal expenses;

Table 2. Cisco: Torpedo Alert Indicators, First Quarter 1999–First Quarter 2001

	1999				2000				2001
Indicators	Q1	Q2	Q3	Q4	Q1	Q2	Q3	Q4	Q1
Earnings quality	NA	NA	NA	NA	NA	NA	NA	NA	NA
Investment quality	A	W	W	W	W	W	A	SA	SA
Cash flow quality	W	A	SA	A	SA	A	A	SA	SA
Valuation	SA	A	A	W	W	W	W	W	SA
Balance sheet quality	NA	NA	NA	NA	NA	NA	NA	W	SA

Note: NA = no alert; W = warning; A = alert; and SA = strong alert.

- maintaining inadequate reserves for inventory or bad debts;
- using a low depreciation rate for assets;
- using balance sheet accounts, such as reserves and allowance for deferred taxes;
- taking write-offs for so called "big bath" pre-merger and in-process R&D items;
- using employee pension plan gains to inflate reported earnings;
- misstating the amounts of liabilities or expenses; and
- using related-party or off-balance-sheet transactions to fund operations or generate income.

Where to Find Them? These aggressive accounting practices can be uncovered in two places. The first place is in the financial statements and in the ratios and time series that can be calculated from the information in them. The second place is in the footnotes to the financial statements. The footnotes can be useful elaborations on the numbers reported in the financial statements. The following are some examples of aggressive accounting practices and how to detect them.

■ *Booking revenues early without earning them.* Often, a company's practice of booking revenues early or without earning them will show up either in accounts receivable or in the company's margins. An example of a company following this practice was Safeskin Corporation, which was a classic 30 percent annual growth company in 1995, 1996, 1997, and into 1998. Safeskin stuffed its inventory channel to make revenue targets, which caused accounts receivable (on a DSO basis) to nearly double from the second to the third quarter of 1998.

■ *Failing to record normal expenses.* A company may fail to record normal expenses, capitalizing them instead. Such a practice could be discovered by a review of either the company's margins or its accrual rate.

Rainbow Technologies provides an example of how this can work. Its reported R&D as a percentage of sales fell from about 10 percent to 6 percent from the first quarter of 1999 to the second quarter of 2000, and reported earnings increased as a result. If the R&D that was capitalized over this time period were added to the R&D expenses for the same period, the actual expenditures for R&D were fairly constant, while the earnings were higher than if all the R&D had been expensed currently. Management justified this treatment as legitimate capitalization of software development costs for a product not yet being sold. This option is acceptable under GAAP under certain circumstances but could be interpreted as an example of aggressive accounting that could have misled some analysts measuring Rainbow's margins.

■ *Maintaining inadequate reserves for inventory or bad debts.* This practice can show up in either of two easily calculated financial ratios: the ratio of bad debt expense to the allowance for bad debts and the ratio of inventory obsolescence expense to the allowance for inventory obsolescence.

Paradyne Networks is an example of a company that used this practice. Paradyne Networks' allowance for bad debts ranged from $3 million to $4 million during the 1997–99 period, but its actual bad debt expense ranged from $6 million to $12 million in the same period. The ratio of Paradyne's allowance for bad debts to receivables fell from the low teens to about 8.7 percent. Paradyne accommodated this difference by reducing revenues rather than increasing bad debt expense or the allowance for bad debts. This accommodation is an unusual treatment but is not unknown and could have masked the problem from a cursory analysis of the accounts as reported.

■ *Using a low depreciation rate for assets.* A company can lower its depreciation rate for assets by lengthening the number of years over which an asset is depreciated. A longer depreciation term means lower depreciation expense and thus higher reported earnings. Cash is not affected. GAAP no longer requires that companies write off their intangibles, but they must test annually the value of intangibles that is reported on the balance sheet. If the asset is no longer worth its value on the balance sheet, the asset must be written down.

King Pharmaceuticals provides an example of how a company's use of a long depreciation life can be used to improve reported earnings. The bulk of King's intangibles is related to the rights to patented drugs that the company buys from other pharmaceutical companies. Although these patents typically have 3–10 years of remaining patent protection, the company claims a longer competitive life and amortization period, often 15–25 years. This claim tends to increase reported earnings, particularly when compared with a 5- or 10-year amortization period.

■ *Balance sheet accounts—reserves and deferred taxes.* The use of certain balance sheet accounts—reserves and deferred taxes—can be a fairly complex accounting strategy. A change in the deferred tax valuation charge, which allows companies the flexibility to either generate current earnings or "store" earnings for some future period can indicate earnings manipulation. For example, a company can take a charge in one period (an expense) to increase its deferred tax valuation account and reverse that charge in later periods, thereby effectively increasing earnings in the latter period.

LaCrosse Footwear serves as a good example of this practice. In 1998 and 1999, LaCrosse recorded no valuation allowance, but in 2000, it recorded a valuation allowance of $22.7 million. By boosting its valuation allowance in 2000 when earnings were strong, the company was able to "save" a portion of those earnings to be reported in future periods.

■ *Taking write-offs—big bath, premerger, in-process R&D.* Taking write-offs can be an aggressive accounting practice and could be the subject of an entire conference. Analysts need to be on the lookout for companies that are "serial chargers"—companies that consistently have large one-time charges. For example, Qwest recently announced a $40-plus billion "big bath" write-down for a significant part of its business, which could potentially boost future earnings. The observant analyst will question any backward-looking comparisons following these kinds of write-downs.

■ *Using employee pension plan gains.* Investment gains earned in employee pension plans in excess of the amount required for funding purposes can be used to increase a company's income and, hence, reported earnings. Verizon Communications, IBM, and General Motors Corporation are three high-profile examples that are discussed by David Zion.[2] Fortunately, this particularly aggressive accounting practice is increasingly being recognized and highlighted by analysts.

■ *Misstating the amounts of liabilities or expenses and using related-party transactions or off-balance-sheet deals.* Finding these practices involves looking at the sources of both income and cash flow in a company's financial statements and reading the disclosures in the financial statement footnotes. Enron's antics provide a classic example, and the diagnosis is discussed in the next section.

Enron

I could not give a presentation on financial reporting issues without talking about Enron. Enron is a prime example of aggressive accounting that lapsed into fraud. Beginning in the second quarter of 1999, the company showed deterioration in all four symptom areas: cash flow quality, balance sheet quality, investment quality, and earnings quality. After the first quarter of 1999 until the third quarter of 2001, the difference between reported and adjusted income (our measure of earnings quality) was substantial in most quarters, as shown in **Figure 3**. As the gap between reported and adjusted earnings grew, reported earnings were not consistently increasing. This fact, combined with the fact that true core earnings were falling, indicated that perhaps all was not well at Enron. The discrepancy between reported and adjusted income that had existed for at least eight quarters increased significantly in the second quarter of 2001, providing a clue to the company's earnings quality problem.

Figure 3. Earnings Quality: Enron, Fourth Quarter 1998–Third Quarter 2001

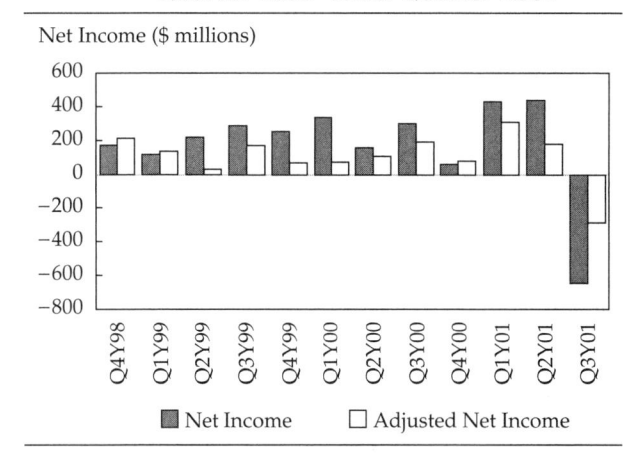

The decline in cash flow quality was also extreme over the same period, as illustrated in **Figure 4**. Notice the huge spike in CFFO in the fourth quarter of 2000; it was approximately 3.5–4.0 times larger than the amount of cash flow Enron had ever reported in one quarter. After that quarter, reported and actual cash flow turned negative. Enron included in operating cash such items as "the proceeds from the sale of merchant assets" and "the receipt of cash associated with the assumption of a contractual obligation." Needless to say, Enron was not exactly Warren Buffett's type of company, with businesses that could be easily understood or easily valued.

Enron's margins, a sign of investment quality, also indicated that problems were brewing. In late

Figure 4. Cash Flow Quality: Enron, Fourth Quarter 1998–Third Quarter 2001

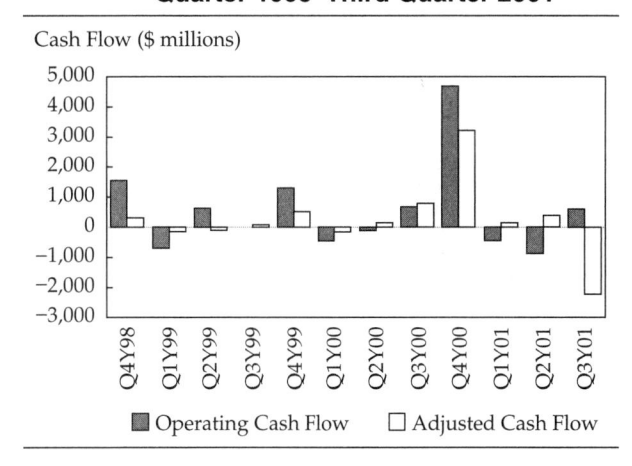

---

[2] Please see Mr. Zion's presentation in this proceedings.

1998, Enron's gross margin was about 9 percent, as shown in **Figure 5**, but by the end of 2000, it was down to about 3 percent and fell rapidly thereafter. As for Enron's ROIC, after hitting a peak of close to 5 percent in the first quarter of 2000 (as shown in **Figure 6**), it fell to about 3.5 percent in the first quarter of 2001 and totally collapsed soon thereafter.

I have not yet discussed valuation, which I liken to taking the fever of a patient, and which is yet another symptom of a corporation's problems. Often, a high valuation of one company relative to another, without consistent supporting financial data to justify the relative valuations, can be a sign that "cult" status has been bestowed on the higher-rated company. Aggressive accounting often becomes the only way for a company's management to maintain the high valuation associated with cult status. Any investment manager comparing Enron and Johnson & Johnson in the 1996–2000 period (before Enron blew up) would have seen that Johnson & Johnson's ROIC was consistently around 25 percent, as shown in **Figure 7**, while Enron was producing an ROIC between 3 percent and 7 percent. Yet at that time, Enron's P/E was about 80 and Johnson & Johnson's P/E was about 30. In valuation terms, Enron's valuation indicated cult status, and this high fever was a further symptom of internal problems.

Figure 5. Margins: Enron, Fourth Quarter 1998–Third Quarter 2001

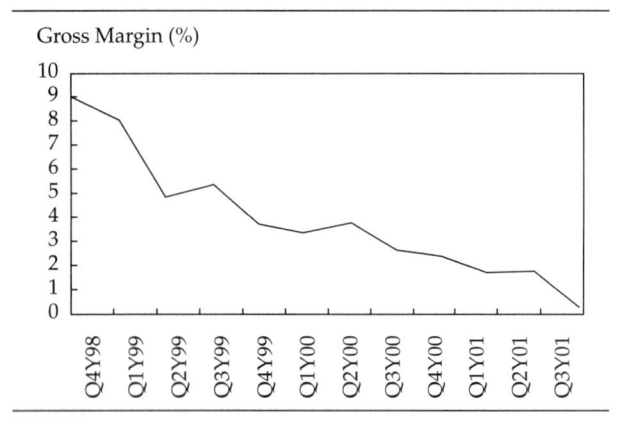

Figure 6. ROIC: Enron, Fourth Quarter 1998–First Quarter 2001

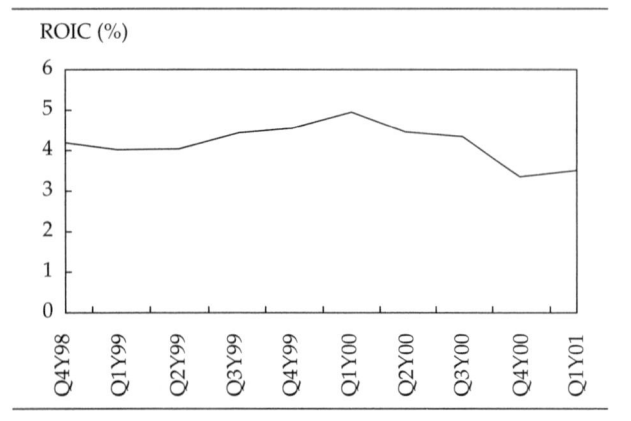

Figure 7. ROIC: Enron and Johnson & Johnson, 1996–2001

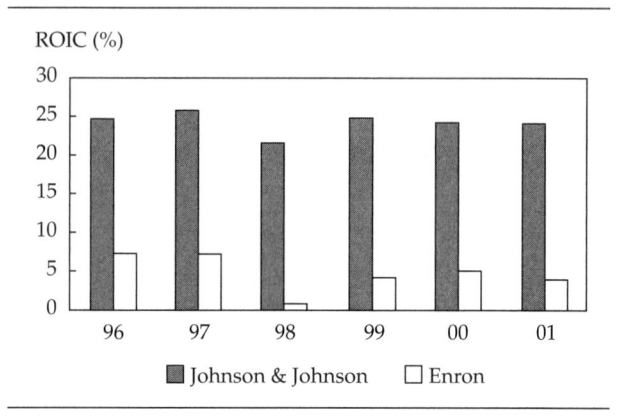

Achieving a Faster, Reliable Diagnosis. First of all, to obtain accurate information from traditional ratio analysis, the data need to be clean. It is imperative that analysts be taught, or that we teach ourselves, techniques to add some new twists to traditional ratio analysis so that we can identify the symptoms of the diseases that are, more often than not, apparent somewhere in the financial statements.

At Jefferson Research & Management, we have our own ways to adjust traditional ratios to remove the effect of GAAP-sanctioned, but often obfuscating, reporting practices reflected in a company's financial statements. We adjust the traditional ratios and time-series indicators, including CFFO, EPS, EPS/CFFO, ROIC, cash flow ROIC, free cash flow, P/E, and price to cash flow. We consider our adjusted ratios to be better indicators than the traditional ratios of the health of a company.

Several resources are available to managers and researchers in their quest to uncover financial reporting problems. Two excellent books by Mulford and Comiskey on the topic are *The Financial Numbers Game* and *The Guide to Financial Reporting and Analysis*.[3] Various data and information services can also be helpful. Standard & Poor's, for example, has a new method of reporting earnings that helps shine a light on some (but not all) aspects of earnings quality. S&P's method adjusts for some of the obfuscating accounting and reporting treatments I have

---
[3]Charles W. Mulford and Eugene E. Comiskey, *The Financial Numbers Game* (New York: John Wiley & Sons, Inc., 2002); Eugene E. Comiskey and Charles W. Mulford, *The Guide to Financial Reporting and Analysis* (New York: John Wiley & Sons, Inc., 2000).

discussed. Some new data services, such as Simplystocks, collect data from a company's financial statement footnotes and supporting schedules, which we use to further decipher a company's financial condition.

Conclusion

Detecting problems in the financial health of a company is not impossible. In fact, as I have described, four diseases are identifiable through a thorough analysis of a company's financial statements and the footnotes to its financial statements. In most cases, some adjustment to the reported numbers will reveal the true health of a company.

Resources exist to help portfolio managers and analysts detect corporate financial ill health, but the entire undertaking requires significant effort and an unwillingness to accept the numbers as reported in the financial statements. Several independent research firms (including our firm) specialize in providing alternative measures and ratings of a company's health that can reduce the effort required to uncover these problems. Whether the research is conducted in-house or outsourced, a disciplined approach to financial analysis should be integrated into the overall investment process to avoid some of the recent accounting and reporting problems that have hurt portfolio performance.

Question and Answer Session

Bruce A. Gulliver, CFA

Question: How do you resist the tendency to believe a company's explanation for why a ratio looks out of line?

Gulliver: Having fallen in love in a world of matchmakers once or twice, believe me, I've learned to rely on the numbers, not the explanation. It has been said that the more defensive a company is, the more likely they are trying to hide something. Remember, the company that was more defensive than any other about its reported numbers was Enron.

Question: Is there a general progression by which a company's financial statement deteriorates, such as starting with the gross margin and progressing to CFFO and then the balance sheet?

Gulliver: It depends on the cause of the deterioration. If several companies in the same industry are facing the same competitive issues, they would likely show the same progression. But if one of the companies decides to go the aggressive route—maybe the company didn't get that big order it expected this quarter—and decides to provide favorable financing to make its goals, the pattern would differ.

Question: What specific adjustments do you make to CFFO?

Gulliver: Cash flow quality should get as much attention as earnings quality, but it generally does not. We take out discontinued items because they are not part of the company's ongoing business. We also take out extraordinary items, which get wide latitude under GAAP, at least as far as the definition of includable items. Wide latitude is one of the reasons that CFFO can be deceptive. In addition, we take out some of the nonoperating items, including the tax benefit from stock options.

Question: Enron was criticized for its poor earnings quality for several years before the company blew up. Why was the company awarded such a high P/E by the market?

Gulliver: I think Enron was a classic example of a company that people wanted to believe in. Analysts wanted to believe that Enron could do things that no company had ever done. Enron had management that people believed in—management that investors believed was smart. It became a cult stock, one of a number of such cult stocks that developed in the late 1990s. Some investors stopped paying attention to the numbers reported by the company and accepted the matchmakers' story that led to the overvaluation.

Question: What do you examine to determine whether an acquisition is likely to be helpful or harmful to a company?

Gulliver: It is particularly useful to look at ROIC and asset turnover to see whether the company is diluting its capital or whether the balance sheet is ballooning because of the acquisition. The numbers reported after the acquisition—after the company's financials have been consolidated—are often telling on this point.

Question: Is a sudden departure from past accounting practices always a red flag that needs to be investigated thoroughly?

Gulliver: Yes. Regardless of the particular change in accounting practice, a sudden departure from past practice is a good indicator that something has fundamentally changed in the company's business situation or its attitude about how it wants to report its financial situation—either more conservatively or more aggressively.

Question: Have you looked at the predictive power of Altman's Z-score as a bankruptcy indicator?

Gulliver: Yes. Altman's Z-score is a reasonably good predictor when a company is right on the edge of bankruptcy. But in my experience, if a company is not in immediate danger of bankruptcy, Altman's Z-score is by itself not a reliable indicator.

Question: Can your approach work on a sector or industry level as opposed to on a one-by-one stock basis?

Gulliver: Yes, if one thinks of a sector as being a composite of many companies. In fact, we produce sector ratings that are a composite of companies within those sectors.

Question: How can you distinguish between margin declines that are symptomatic of the downturn in the economy as opposed to margin declines that are the result of previous aggressive accounting practices?

Gulliver: For the purpose of understanding where the company's stock price might be going and the company's fundamental strength, the source of margin declines doesn't matter. Regardless of what causes a company's margins to fall—a competitive situation or an aggressive accounting situation—it is still bad news for the company's fundamentals and its stock price. It is sometimes difficult to distinguish between the two diseases because the indicators overlap, but earnings quality problems are more likely to show up in cash flow and balance sheet measures.

Question: Will senior management's certification of the financial statements have a material effect on reporting practices?

Gulliver: We debated this question in-house and did not reach a consensus. I believe that a financial officer or a CEO of a company has to at least seriously consider whether he or she thinks the financial statements are accurate and not misleading. No empirical evidence at this point exists to support that conclusion, but I think the certification requirement will have a positive impact on reporting practices. Senior managers have to sign on the bottom line, knowing that they face potential legal consequences for a misleading or fraudulent representation.

Question: Could you go into more detail regarding the deferred tax valuation account?

Gulliver: The deferred tax valuation account issue is complicated. Look for changes that occur in the deferred tax valuation account and how those changes flow through the income statement. Again, much of the treatment is totally legitimate from a GAAP perspective. Essentially, companies are making a forecast about the future and estimating whether or not they should be able to realize the anticipated tax benefits associated with those forecasts, which, in turn, involves forecasting a taxable earnings position.

Question: Does the lack of standardization of terms inhibit or impede analysts from making accurate valuations?

Gulliver: Yes, more standardization of accounting terms and treatments would make financial analysis much easier. The number of definitions that a company can use for the allowance for bad debts, for example, is significant, according to one expert I have consulted. Maybe 10 or 15 different possible definitions exist for the same accounting term, which makes financial analysis complex. Similarly, companies have fairly wide latitude in accounting treatments for many items, including bad debt allowances and expenses and other items I mentioned in this presentation.

Question: If the U.S. accounting system had more of an emphasis on the principles (as in Europe), would we get less tripped up by the rules?

Gulliver: Whether emphasizing principles is better than emphasizing rules is an interesting argument. In both cases, a company's senior managers (and the accountants) still have to make judgments. We're probably not going to devise a prescription that will give us the perfect numbers all the time, even if we could all agree on the definition of "perfect" numbers. Using principles rather than rules could possibly better advance the cause, but I'm not sure.

The Magic of Pension Accounting

David A. Zion, CFA
*Accounting and Tax Policy Analyst
Credit Suisse First Boston
New York City*

> The decline in equity markets and record-low interest rates have had a negative impact on the health of defined-benefit pension plans. Confusing accounting, complicated funding requirements, and pension obligations with unknown future cash flows further contribute to investor anxiety. Measuring and analyzing a company's potential exposure to its pension plan can provide valuable information for analysts and investors alike.

Concern is rising that the smoothing mechanisms originally designed to reduce reported earnings volatility in Statement of Financial Accounting Standards (SFAS) No. 87, *Employers' Accounting for Pensions*, have led to misleading financial statements.[1] Investors want to know which companies and industries have the most exposure to defined-benefit pension plans, how large a claim the pension plan has on their stake in the company, and to what extent the exposure to the pension plan affects earnings and balance sheets. In addition, investors are concerned about the increase in cash contributions that the companies would have to make to their pension plans if their funded status continues to decline. Standard & Poor's (S&P) is evaluating the potential credit-rating implications, and in a worst-case scenario, some companies could be forced into bankruptcy.

To measure and analyze such pension exposure, Bill Carcache and I, in our recently released report "The Magic of Pension Accounting," looked at the data on S&P 500 companies with defined-benefit plans, analyzing the data from a number of different angles, which included forecasting future results using our pension forecast model.[2] In this presentation, to answer the simple question of which company has the most exposure to pension issues, I will focus on four types of exposure: shareholder exposure, balance sheet exposure, earnings exposure, and cash flow exposure. I will also discuss our methodology for replacing the magic of pension accounting with each plan's economic reality. Furthermore, I will talk about quality of earnings and the pension plan, along with key assumptions, particularly the expected return assumption.

Why Pension Accounting?

Why do investors have so many questions about pension accounting? I believe most of this uncertainty can be attributed to three sources of confusion and to the recent changes in the markets.

Sources of Confusion. First, the accounting methods are extremely confusing. Even the terminology in SFAS No. 87 is confusing. Service costs, interest costs, unrecognized gains and losses, projected benefit obligation—what do these terms mean? Additionally, the smoothing mechanisms that are built into SFAS No. 87 further complicate the accounting. Often, the reporting does not accurately reflect the economics of the pension plan, which throws investors for a loop.

Second, pension plans have extremely complicated funding requirements, which has not been a significant issue until recently. For healthy plans, funding requirements are not that important. But all of a sudden, the health of pension plans has deteriorated as a result of low interest rates and a weak equity market, and companies are facing the need to fund their pension plans. The funding requirements are buried in the tax code. They are part of the ERISA regulations and are found in U.S. Internal Revenue Code (IRC) Section 412. Anyone who thinks SFAS

---

[1] For a summary of SFAS No. 87, please see Appendix A.
[2] David A. Zion, CFA, and Bill Carcache, "The Magic of Pension Accounting," Credit Suisse First Boston (27 September 2002). To download a PDF of this report, go to www.eric.org/issue-briefs/download/pension_accounting.pdf.

No. 87 is confusing should take a look at IRC Section 412.

Finally, the "mysterious economics" of pension plans, as I refer to them, create even more confusion. A defined-benefit pension plan has a series of unknown future cash flow obligations. To estimate these unknown cash flow obligations, actuaries need to make a number of assumptions.

When all three factors—confusing accounting, complicated funding requirements, and mysterious economics—are mixed together, the reason I get so many questions about pension accounting becomes clear.

Recent Changes in the Markets. The need to understand pension accounting has certainly intensified recently because of the market environment over the past few years. The combination of a decline in the equity markets and low interest rates has been a double whammy for companies in the S&P 500 Index that have defined-benefit pension plans, as shown in **Figure 1**. Declining equity markets have forced pension plan assets lower, and low interest rates have forced the projected benefit obligation (PBO) higher. This environment, by definition, is bad for defined-benefit pension plans and results in lower assets and higher obligations.

As Figure 1 shows, the last time that defined-benefit plans were underfunded in the aggregate was 1993, and they were only minimally underfunded. The situation looked great until 1999, when defined-benefit plans were funded at about 130 percent, which translates into approximately $250 billion in overfunding. But in the past two years (from 1999 to the end of 2001), that overfunding has disappeared. So, at the end of 2001, the defined-benefit plans in the S&P 500 had, in aggregate, about $1 trillion in assets and $1 trillion in obligations. Where did that $250 billion go? Roughly $80 billion disappeared with the decline in the market value of pension plan assets, and the other $170 billion disappeared as a result of the increase in the value of the PBOs, which are highly sensitive to changes in interest rates. That is, low interest rates forced the pension obligations much higher over the course of the two-year period. We estimate that at the end of 2002, the defined-benefit pension plans for S&P 500 companies will be underfunded by about $240 billion.

Who Has Exposure?

A common question asked by investors is: Who has exposure to defined-benefit pension plans? An examination of the companies in the S&P 500, which contains a good cross-section of companies, can help answer this question. The companies in the S&P 500 can be split into two groups: those *with* defined-benefit pension plans and those *without* defined-benefit pension plans.

Companies without Defined-Benefit Pension Plans. For the most part, these companies offer defined-contribution plans. Compared with defined-benefit pension plans, the economics of defined-contribution plans are simple and the accounting is straightforward. In a defined-contribution plan, the company has promised a specific contribution into the plan on behalf of its employees. For example, in a 401(k) plan in which the company matches the contribution that the employee makes, once the company matches the contribution, its obligation is complete until the next matching date. The contributing

Figure 1. Funded Status of Defined-Benefit Pension Plans of S&P 500 Companies, 1991–2004

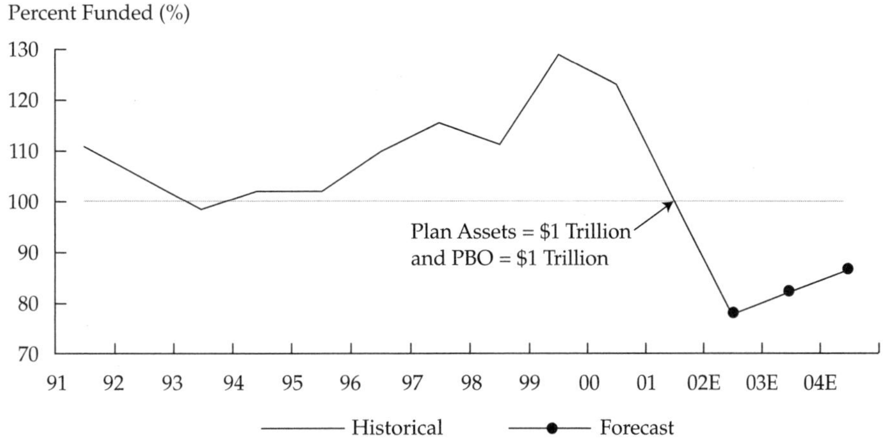

Sources: Based on company data and CSFB estimates.

company accounts for the transaction by reporting an expense on its income statement.

Of all the companies in the S&P 500, 140 do not have defined-benefit pension plans. (To see this list of 140 companies, please see Appendix A of our report "The Magic of Pension Accounting.") Generally, these are new companies, technology companies, and nonunionized companies (such as Cisco Systems, Dell Computer Corporation, Microsoft Corporation, and Oracle Corporation). Most of these companies, however, do tend to have another employee benefit issue: employee stock options.

Companies with Defined-Benefit Pension Plans. If 140 companies in the S&P 500 do not have defined-benefit pension plans, the other 360 companies do. These plans are the focus of my presentation (and of our report).

In a defined-benefit pension plan, the employer has promised to pay a future benefit to its retired employees using a benefit formula. For example, the employer may promise to pay its retired employees some percentage of the employees' final-year(s) salaries throughout the remainder of the employees' lifetimes. The employer accepts all of the investment risk as a result of this structure. If the assets are not there to support the payment of the benefit, the payment of that benefit will reduce the employer's cash flow. Defined-benefit pension plans are typically found in older companies, unionized companies, and industrial companies. Thus, 360 companies in the S&P 500 have, or could have, a pension problem.

Some industries are more exposed to defined-benefit plans than others. Every aerospace and defense company in the S&P 500 has a defined-benefit pension plan. And all S&P 500 companies in the auto, auto component, paper and forest products, and road and rail sectors (again, old line, unionized, industrialized types of industries) have defined-benefit plans. At the opposite end of the spectrum are the S&P 500 companies in the wireless telecommunications, software, semiconductor equipment, and Internet sectors, which do not have defined-benefit pension plans.

Measuring and Analyzing Exposure

To measure the exposure of these companies to their defined-benefit pension plans, we analyzed the data from several angles. First, we projected for the next three years the pension costs, funded status, and funding requirements according to the tax code for each of these companies. To make these forecasts, we used the publicly available information from the companies' 10-K forms and made a number of simplifying assumptions.

The second approach we used was to treat each pension plan as an investment subsidiary. That is, we put each pension plan on the balance sheet, reporting the pension plan's assets as an asset and the PBO as a liability. Additionally, we removed the smoothing mechanisms from the income statement and instead recorded what actually happened in the pension plan.

Furthermore, we analyzed each pension plan's publicly disclosed actuarial assumptions: the expected rate of return on plan assets, the discount rate, and the salary inflation rate.

Another approach we used was to analyze 10 years of historical data, and yet another was to create what we refer to as a "pension report card" to grade the exposures that companies had to their defined-benefit pension plans grouped by industry.

We found that most of the 360 companies with defined-benefit plans do not have significant exposure to their plans. We then split the companies that do have high exposure to their pension plans into two groups: companies with *overfunded* pension plans and companies with *underfunded* pension plans.

Overfunded Plans. For the most part, the risks for companies with overfunded plans are limited to earnings. Companies with overfunded pension plans generally report pension plan income on their income statement. But as the health of the pension plan deteriorates, the pension plan's income can decline; therefore, the company's earnings can decline. These companies also have quality-of-earnings issues. Again, the problem is determining the pension plan's contribution to the bottom line or margins. The industries that tend to have overfunded plans are diversified telecommunications (e.g., the baby Bells), paper and forest products, and industrial conglomerates. General Electric Company, for example, has a highly overfunded pension plan.

Underfunded Plans. For companies with underfunded pension plans, the risks are more troublesome. Like companies with overfunded plans, companies with underfunded plans have earnings-related issues. These companies tend to report pension expense on their income statement. As the health of the pension plan deteriorates, the company may report higher pension expense, lowering its earnings. More important, the company may have to begin to fund its pension plan. That is, cash may have to come out of shareholders' pockets and go into the pension plan. These companies' balance sheets could also take a beating. Furthermore, an underfunded pension plan can have implications for a company's credit rating. Thus, companies with underfunded pension plans have a broader set of troublesome issues to face than do companies with overfunded pension plans. The sectors that fall into the underfunded camp should be no surprise—autos, auto components, and airlines.

Types of Exposure

In our analysis, we specifically evaluated the effects of four types of exposure: shareholder exposure, balance sheet exposure, earnings exposure, and cash flow exposure.

Shareholder Exposure. We wanted to measure how much of a claim the pension plan has on a shareholders' stake in the company. To find this measure, we forecast the amount that a pension plan could be underfunded at the end of 2002, and we compared this amount with the company's market cap. We found that for 30 companies in the S&P 500, the pension plan would be underfunded by more than 25 percent of the company's market cap. In other words, the pension plan may have a claim on more than a quarter of the shareholder's stake in the company. For example, we estimated that at the end of 2002, General Motors Corporation's (GM's) pension plan would be underfunded by $29 billion, compared with a market cap of $21 billion. So, the amount the pension plan is underfunded is actually greater than the company's market cap. Clearly, the pension plan participants and the plan have a significant claim on a shareholder's stake in GM. Conversely, we estimated that for 212 companies, the amount the pension plan will be underfunded represents less than 5 percent of the company's market cap. Thus, some companies have a lot of exposure to their pension plans, but most of them do not.

Another way we tried to measure shareholder exposure was to analyze the pension obligation. We forecast the pension obligation at the end of 2002 and compared this amount with the company's market cap. The point is that a company may have pension assets today but those pension assets may not be there tomorrow. We found 31 companies in which the pension obligation was greater than the company's market cap, which means significant potential exposure for the company's shareholders. For 94 companies, the pension obligation was less than 5 percent of the company's market cap. So, based on analysis of the PBO, a large number of companies have only limited exposure to their pension plans.

Balance Sheet Exposure. To evaluate the balance sheet exposure, we forecast the minimum pension liability, which is the excess of the accumulated benefit obligation (ABO) over the fair value of the pension plan assets. Historically, the minimum pension liability has been a nonissue for most companies, but as the health of pension plans has deteriorated, it is becoming more important. For example, GM took a $9.5 billion charge to reflect the minimum pension liability on its balance sheet during 2001.

By instituting the minimum pension liability requirement, the Financial Accounting Standards Board (FASB) basically created a floor on the liability that a company has to record on its balance sheet for the pension plan. If the pension liability on the balance sheet is lower than the company's minimum pension liability, the company must record an additional pension liability on its balance sheet, potentially taking a charge to shareholders' equity. For example, assume that the minimum pension liability for a company is $500 and that the pension liability on the balance sheet is only $200. The company has to record an additional liability on the balance sheet for the difference between the two, or $300.

Companies are now running into this problem quite often. From talking to actuaries, I understand that the most common question they hear from their clients is: Will we have to take a minimum pension liability charge? Several companies have recently made announcements about taking this additional liability charge. Lucent Technologies, The Boeing Company, and Maytag Corporation all recently announced a charge against equity to record the minimum pension liability. Their hits to equity are expected to be $3 billion, $4 billion, and $114 million, respectively.

Thus, we estimated the charge to equity to record the minimum pension liability and compared it with the company's shareholders' equity. We found that for 26 companies, the charge to equity would be 25 percent or more of their total equity at the end of 2001. The resulting problem is that such a large charge to equity can cause the company to trip over debt covenants. So, even though the minimum pension liability charge is a noncash accounting entry, it has the potential to produce serious financial ramifications for companies that are forced to make the adjustment.

Earnings Exposure. To determine the earnings exposure of a company with an underfunded pension plan, we estimated the pension cost for the next three years for all the companies in the S&P 500 with defined-benefit pension plans. The base case assumptions we made to estimate the pension costs of these companies are shown in Panel A of **Table 1**. Panel B shows the aggregate findings based on these assumptions. Accounting pension income in 2001 was $7 billion, but our estimate is actually an expense (an accounting pension expense) of $1 billion for 2002

Table 1. Summary of Base Case Assumptions and Aggregate Findings

	2001	2002E	2003E
A. Base case assumptions			
Plan assets			
Equities—65%		–18.85%	10.00%
Fixed income—35%		8.00%	5.50%
Actual return	–7.50%	–9.45%	8.43%
Projected discount rate change (bps)		–50	25
Inflation		3%	3%
B. Aggregate findings (US$ billions, except percent funded)			
Percent funded	100%	79%	82%
Funded status	$4	–$243	–$206
Accounting pension income (expense)	$7	–$1	–$15
Real pension income (expense)	–$224	–$259	$7
Cash contributions	$15	$10	$29

Sources: Based on company data and CSFB estimates.

and an expense of $15 billion for 2003. Note that our estimates for 2002 and 2003 were calculated using the same expected return assumption used in 2001.

To determine which companies' future earnings are exposed to their pension plans, we compared the change in earnings that would be associated with the estimated 2002 and 2003 pension costs with the company's First Call consensus earnings estimate for 2003. We found 27 companies in which the increase in pension cost accounts for at least 10 percent of their 2003 consensus earnings estimate. For example, we estimated the increase in The Goodyear Tire and Rubber Company's pension cost per share from 2002 to 2003 to be 53 cents. At the time we did this analysis, the First Call consensus earnings number for Goodyear in 2003 was 74 cents. So, the change in pension cost divided by the First Call consensus earnings number (53 cents divided by 74 cents) is 72 percent; hence, the estimated increase in pension cost for 2003 could account for about 72 percent of the consensus estimate. The question then is: How much of this increase in pension cost is already factored into that consensus number? I do not know the answer. For some companies, this expectation is reflected in earnings estimates; for some it is not. The answer depends on the analyst, the company, and the historical importance of the pension plan to the company.

We believe the expected return assumptions will be revised downward across the board sometime in the near future. For S&P 500 companies, the median expected return assumption on pension plan assets was 9.2 percent for 2001. We expect it to drop 50–100 bps, settling around 8.5 percent. And if the expected return assumption does fall, earnings will fall along with it. For the entire S&P 500, if the expected return assumption drops 100 bps, earnings will fall by $10 billion based on our model. A back-of-the-envelope method to determine the impact on earnings from a change in the expected return assumption is to multiply the change in the expected return assumption by the market value of plan assets. For example, the S&P 500 has $1 trillion in pension plan assets, so a drop of 1 percent in the expected return assumption reduces earnings by about $10 billion ($1 trillion × 1 percent).

Table 2 shows the 10 companies whose earnings have the most sensitivity to changes in the expected return assumption. For example, without a change in its expected return assumption, Northrop Grumman Corporation would be expected to have $2.52 per share in pension income in 2003. Dropping the return assumption by 100 bps produces only $1.34 per share of pension income. If Northrop Grumman lowers its return assumption to 6.5 percent, it will have pension expense, rather than pension income, of $1.03 per share.

Cash Flow Exposure. The cash flow exposure is probably the most important of all the types of exposure a company has to its pension plan because it has real valuation implications. In valuing a corporation, investors are forecasting a series of future cash flows and discounting them back to the present. If a company is required to contribute to its pension plan, cash flows to investors are reduced; therefore, the corporation's valuation declines.

■ *Contributions.* Contributions to a defined-benefit pension plan do not have to be in the form of cash. For example, contributions can come in the form of company stock as long as the stock does not exceed 10 percent of the pension plan's assets (an

Table 2. Estimated Pension (Income) Expense per Share for 2003 Based on Changing Return Assumptions

Company	Base Case	Down 100 bps	Assuming 6.5% Return
Northrop Grumman Corp.	−$2.52	−$1.34	$1.03
General Motors Corp.	5.83	6.51	7.83
U.S. Steel Corp.	−0.57	0.05	0.91
TRW	0.04	0.47	1.10
Delta Air Lines	3.75	4.12	5.04
Lockheed Martin Corp.	0.02	0.35	1.01
Cummins	0.74	1.05	1.82
Boeing Co.	−0.18	0.11	0.61
NCR Corp.	−0.36	−0.08	0.54
Navistar International Corp.	1.24	1.49	2.08

Sources: Based on company data and CSFB estimates.

ERISA rule). We estimate that for all the companies in the S&P 500 with defined-benefit plans, the required contribution to those pension plans in 2003 will be about $29 billion, double the actual contribution in 2001. According to our estimates, GM will have the largest increase in contributions. GM contributed $191 million to its pension plan in 2001, and we estimate that the company will have to add another $5 billion to its pension plan in 2003. GM, however, has said it does not have to put that $5 billion into its pension plan in 2003 because it has an ERISA funding credit that will offset its required contribution. This credit does not eliminate the liability but simply pushes it further into the future; thus, we did not take the credit into account when we forecasted GM's contributions.

■ *Funding requirements.* A major simplifying assumption for this analysis is that forecasted contributions are calculated based on U.S. funding requirements. This simplifying assumption is crucial because the funding requirements for international pension plans are completely different from those for U.S. plans.

To determine the annual pension funding requirements, we performed a four-part analysis for each company: the minimum funding requirement, the additional funding requirement, the Pension Benefit Guaranty Corporation (PBGC) variable premium, and the maximum contribution.

- *Minimum funding requirement.* Companies with overfunded pension plans do not have to make a contribution. Companies with underfunded pension plans contribute the normal cost (think compensation cost) plus the unfunded obligation amortized over 5–30 years.
- *Additional funding requirement.* The additional funding requirement is probably the most important driver of cash contributions to the pension plan. Under the additional funding requirement, the company must pay the amount of underfunding to the pension plan over a short time period (typically 3–5 years). The length of this payback period depends on the company's level of underfunding. The more severely underfunded a company is, the faster the company must make up the shortfall.

The additional funding requirement has become a hot-button issue for a number of companies because the requirement kicks in once the pension plan becomes less than 90 percent funded, although companies are provided with several grace periods. The problem is that the funded status of the pension plan that determines the funding requirements differs from the information in the pension footnote. In an ideal world, companies would disclose their plans' funded status according to the tax code in the pension footnote.

- *PBGC variable premium.* The PBGC, which pays retirees' pensions if their employer fails, requires that underfunded pension plans pay an additional premium based on the amount of underfunding. The PBGC variable premium is important because the threat of having to pay this premium spurs companies to make contributions to their pension plans. The premium paid to the PBGC for an underfunded plan is money spent, but alternatively, if the company uses this money to make a contribution to its pension plan, the money remains "in-house." Many companies are wrestling with this problem: Do we write the check to PBGC, or do we write a larger check to our pension plan?

- *Maximum contribution.* The maximum contribution is the maximum amount a company can contribute to its plan in a taxable year and still be able to deduct the entire amount in the calculation of its income taxes. The maximum contribution for an underfunded pension plan is the amount needed to make the plan fully funded. Companies with overfunded plans cannot deduct contributions to the plans on their tax return. Any contributions that exceed the maximum get hit with a 10 percent excise tax. Thus, companies with overfunded pension plans generally do not continue to contribute to their plans.

Excising the Accounting Magic

Pension accounting should be simple, but unfortunately, it is quite complicated. To simplify our analysis, we made adjustments to the balance sheets and income statements of the companies we were evaluating to better represent the economic realities of pension accounting. We put the pension plan on the balance sheet in two pieces—the market value of the assets as an asset and the PBO as a liability—and we put the actual return from the pension plan assets on the income statement, along with changes in the pension obligation. Next, we sliced pension cost into several pieces, as opposed to recording one net number on the income statement, as is done today.

Placing the pension plan on the balance sheet makes some companies look like equal parts pension plan and operating company. For example, Lucent's assets almost double when its pension plan assets are put on its balance sheet. Furthermore, when the pension obligation is treated as debt, the debt of some companies increases dramatically. For 16 of the 360 S&P 500 companies with defined-benefit plans, debt increases by more than 200 percent when the pension obligation is put on the balance sheet.

Figure 2 shows in the aggregate the difference between the "real" pension cost and the pension accounting cost. The pension accounting cost (the solid line) includes all the smoothing mechanisms allowed under SFAS No. 87. Clearly, these smoothing mechanisms work well, because the solid line is indeed quite smooth, particularly in comparison with the dotted line, which shows the "real" cost.

The underlying volatility of the market value of a pension plan becomes apparent by observing the actual return on pension plan assets (i.e., by eliminating smoothing). For the entire universe of S&P 500 companies with defined-benefit plans, eliminating smoothing in 2001 would have reduced earnings by about 69 percent. In 2000, it would have reduced earnings by about 10 percent, and in 1999, by about 25 percent. For 82 companies, earnings would have dropped more than 50 percent in 2001 if smoothing was eliminated, and for 7 companies, net income would have dropped more than $5 billion.

Figure 2. Pension Accounting Cost vs. "Real" Pension Cost, 1999–2004
(US$ billions)

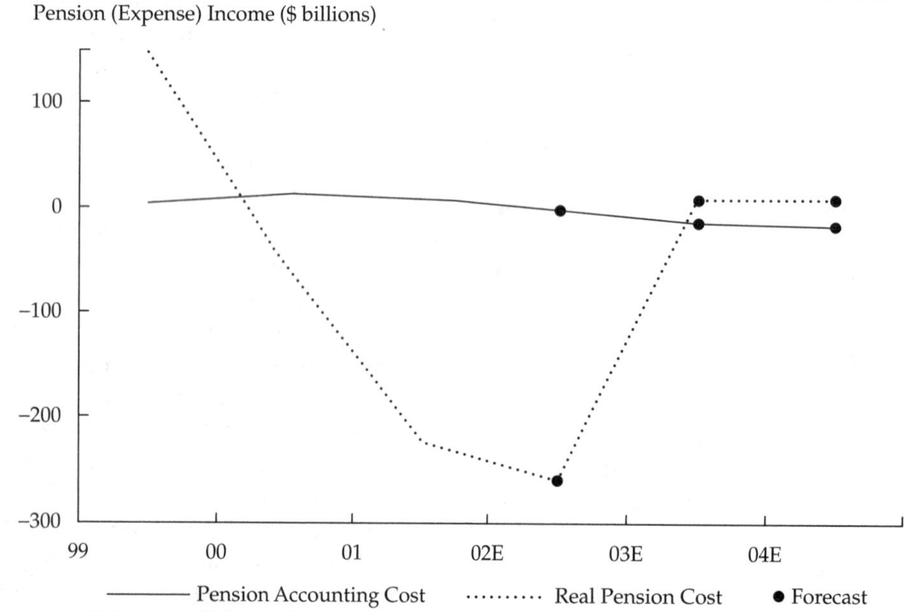

Sources: Based on company data and CSFB estimates.

The components of net pension cost, which include service cost, interest cost, and expected return on plan assets, are combined and reported as part of operating income. Net pension cost is reported wherever the company reports labor cost, generally cost of goods sold or sales, general, and administrative costs, but companies do not usually disclose where it is reported. We adjusted operating income to include only the service cost component (what we refer to as the "real compensation cost" associated with the pension plan) on the income statement. After making this adjustment for 2001, 59 companies had an operating income drop of about 10 percent. Margins are also affected. In 2001, nine companies' margins dropped by more than 400 bps after this adjustment.

We made the same sort of adjustments to enterprise value (EV) and earnings before interest, taxes, depreciation, and amortization (EBITDA). That is, we treated the underfunded status of the pension plan as net debt (if a plan was underfunded, this adjustment would increase the EV, and if it was overfunded, it would reduce the EV) and we removed pension cost and replaced it with service cost. Then, we recalculated the EV/EBITDA multiples on a historical basis. For seven companies, this multiple rose by more than 30 percent.

Quality of Earnings

A central concern of investors is determining how much of a company's earnings and margins can be attributed to the pension plan. To ascertain the true impact of a pension plan on a company's quality of earnings, the following questions should always be asked:

- What percentage of net income is pension income?
- How much of the growth in earnings is from rising pension income?
- How much of the growth in earnings is from declining pension costs?

Of the 360 S&P 500 companies with defined-benefit plans, 19 had more than 20 percent of their bottom line enhanced by the income earned from their pension plans in 2001. For example, in 2001 (admittedly a tough year for many companies), 204 percent of Verizon Communications' net income came from its pension plan. In both 1999 and 2000, 21 percent of Verizon's bottom line came from its pension plan. The pension plan's impact on the quality of earnings of a number of companies has been a consistent concern.

Expected Return Assumption

Companies make various assumptions when accounting for their pension plans, and changes in these assumptions naturally affect the health of the plan and the company. **Exhibit 1** shows the various effects of these changes.

The expected return assumption seems to get the most attention. When a company changes its expected return assumption, the change affects neither the value of its pension assets nor the funded status of its pension plan, but it does affect earnings. If a company increases its expected return assumption, earnings will increase. If a company reduces its expected return assumption, earnings will decrease.

As I said previously, expected return assumptions are falling across the board. Bank of America is talking about lowering its expected return assumption from 9.5 percent to 8.5 percent, and Cummins is

Exhibit 1. Impact of Changes in Assumptions

	Off-Balance-Sheet Items			Net Pension Cost Components			
Assumption/ Change	Fair Market Value of Plan Assets	PBO	Funded Status	Service Cost	Interest Cost	Expected Return	Net Pension Cost
Discount rate							
Increase	None	Decrease	Favorable	Decrease	Increase	None	Decrease
Decrease	None	Increase	Unfavorable	Increase	Decrease	None	Increase
Expected rate of return							
Increase	None	None	None	None	None	Increase	Decrease
Decrease	None	None	None	None	None	Decrease	Increase
Salary inflation rate							
Increase	None	Increase	Unfavorable	Increase	None	None	Increase
Decrease	None	Decrease	Favorable	Decrease	None	None	Decrease

Source: Based on CSFB estimates.

talking about dropping from 10 percent to 8.5 percent. **Table 3** lists the companies in the S&P 500 that were using an expected return assumption of more than 10 percent in 2001.

We assumed plans had a mix of 65 percent equity/35 percent fixed income. That assumption is based on the findings of a Greenwich Associates survey of 1,400 pension plans. For our sample of S&P 500 companies, we compared the actual return with the expected return on the company's pension assets. Panel A of **Table 4** shows the three companies in the S&P 500 whose actual return on their defined-benefit plans' assets exceeded their expected return in 2001. These pension plans are either well managed or have a conservative pension asset allocation mix.

Panel B shows the companies with the widest negative spread between actual and expected return. Bank of New York Company, for example, expected to earn 10.5 percent on its pension assets in 2001. Its actual return was a loss of 31.63 percent. The implication is that Bank of New York has an aggressive pension plan portfolio.

Conclusion

The accounting for pension plans, defined-benefit plans in particular, is complicated. At times, the numbers appear to have been created by "magic." Thus, analysts and investors are justifiably confused.

Ultimately, investors (and hence analysts) are concerned about investors' exposure to these plans. Although underfunded plans pose the greatest liability, overfunded plans can also negatively affect investors if the pension plan is contributing a disproportionate share to the company's bottom line—misleading investors into thinking the company is healthier than it is.

In examining the data on S&P 500 companies from various angles, Bill Carcache and I focused on four types of exposure: shareholder exposure, balance sheet exposure, earnings exposure, and cash flow exposure. To identify this exposure, we had to make various accounting and reporting adjustments and a number of simplifying assumptions. The bad news is that some companies are heavily exposed to their pension plans; the good news is that the majority are not.

Table 3. Expected Return Assumptions by Year for Companies with Assumptions Greater than 10 Percent in 2001

Company	2001	2000	1999
Freeport McMoran Copper & Gold	12.00%	12.00%	NA
U.S. Bancorp	11.00	12.15	11.38%
Weyerhaeuser Co.	11.00	11.50	11.50
FedEx Corp.	10.90	10.90	10.90
PPG Industries	10.90	10.90	10.90
Lehman Brothers Holdings	10.81	10.88	9.19
Illinois Tool Works	10.51	10.55	9.68
Bank of New York Co.	10.50	10.50	10.50
Coors (Adolph)–C1 B	10.50	10.50	10.50
Guidant Corp.	10.50	NA	NA
Harley-Davidson	10.50	10.50	10.30
Kellogg Co.	10.50	10.40	10.40
Lilly (Eli) & Co.	10.50	10.50	10.50
Sysco Corp.	10.50	10.50	10.50
Darden Restaurants	10.40	10.40	10.40
General Mills	10.40	10.40	10.40
FirstEnergy Corp.	10.25	10.25	10.25
Engelhard Corp.	10.04	NA	NA

NA = not available.

Sources: Based on company data and CSFB estimates.

Table 4. Widest Spreads between Expected and Actual Return Rates in 2001

Company	Expected Rate of Return	Actual Return
A. Widest positive spreads		
SLM Corp.	10.00%	13.21%
Merrill Lynch & Co.	6.60	7.90
Loews Corp.	8.25	8.61
B. Widest negative spreads		
Bank of New York Co.	10.50%	–31.63%
Harley-Davidson	10.50	–25.46
Allstate Corp.	9.50	–23.27
Gannett Co.	10.00	–22.15
PepsiCo	9.80	–20.35
Schwab (Charles) Corp.	9.00	–21.13
Raytheon Co.	9.50	–20.54

Sources: Based on company data and CSFB estimates.

Question and Answer Session

David A. Zion, CFA

Question: Does a recognized source exist for your data?

Zion: A lot of the historical data came from Compustat, which does a good job of gathering this information. But we found a few wrinkles. For example, if a company provides a range rather than a single data point, Compustat will automatically default to "NA" (not available), so we had to adjust for that problem.

Compustat gathers most of the basic information: pension plan assets, obligations, and reported pension costs. It gathers the three company-disclosed assumptions—the expected return rate, the discount rate, and the salary inflation rate. It also gathers some of the components of pension cost—service cost, interest cost, and expected return on assets. It doesn't gather the detailed reconciliations behind the changes in the assets and the changes in the obligations. We had to search the 10-K for each of the 360 S&P 500 companies with defined-benefit pension plans and pull out that information by hand, which was a painful process. So, Compustat is picking up a good amount of information, but it is not picking up all of the information.

Question: Is there an observed correlation between the assumed rate of return and the asset mix?

Zion: The existence of any correlation would depend on the year you are analyzing. Maybe you could argue that there was some correlation in 2001 because the companies in Table 4 with the widest negative spreads had high expected rates of return. Thus, those companies' pension funds may have been heavily weighted toward equities. The median expected return assumption was about 9.2 percent for the S&P 500, ranging from a low of around 6 percent to a high of 12 percent. In general, at the bottom of that spectrum are companies that are heavily allocated to fixed income and at the top are companies heavily allocated to equity.

Companies don't disclose their asset allocation information, although it would be valuable information. There are probably three or four disclosures that are missing. The pension footnote disclosure contains some of the best information you can get your hands on in the financial statements because it is consistent from one company to the next. But what is missing is the mix of pension assets, the accumulated benefit obligation, and the contribution to the pension plan. The footnote states the amount of the contribution, but what was it? Was it cash? Was it stocks? Companies aren't going to go out of their way to provide that information unless they're required to disclose it.

Question: Why are certain industries underfunded and others overfunded?

Zion: The industries that have underfunded pension plans tend to be unionized industries. At these companies, defined-benefit pension plans are still being offered to new employees. So, the obligation continues to grow as they keep adding new employees to the plan.

But for a lot of companies, particularly nonunionized companies, defined-benefit pension plans are a legacy issue. They're not being offered to new employees. New employees are offered defined-contribution plans. So, over time, this funding issue is becoming less and less of a problem because defined-benefit pension plans are being phased out by a number of companies.

Question: How does a pension buyout work?

Zion: Employees' pensions are obligations having a series of future cash flows. With a buyout, the corporation tries to settle the obligations immediately by making a lump-sum cash payment to the employees (to the extent that the employees and the union accept it). By making this lump-sum cash payment, the company wipes out some portion of its total pension obligation.

From an accounting perspective, once the buyout is completed, gains and losses that hadn't been recognized in the past are now recognized. A buyout may be one option for companies to alleviate some of the problems associated with their pension plans; ultimately, it depends on whether the employees and the unions accept the buyout offer.

Question: How can pension assets be reported without misleading investors into believing that those assets are available to pay creditors or other operating expenses?

Zion: In our report, we tried to address the problem from an exposure perspective, which is why we made the financial statement adjustments that we did: We put the plan assets on the balance sheet as an asset and we put the obligation on the balance sheet as a liability. In reality, however, the company cannot use pension assets to pay bills. Pension assets are solely for the benefit of the pension plan participants. Another way of approaching the problem is on a net basis. If the pension plan is overfunded, record the overfunded amount as an asset. If the pension plan is underfunded, record the underfunded amount as a liability.

Either method is better than the situation we find ourselves in today, in which the pension assets and liabilities reported on the balance sheet are totally misleading. The accounting rules have to change. I wouldn't be surprised if the FASB turns its attention to pension accounting in the near future. Initially, the FASB will probably put the pension plan on the financial statements. It is just a matter of whether it should be reported on a gross or net basis.

Question: Do defense contractors get special treatment for their pension plans?

Zion: For defense contractors, a pension shortfall is likely to be passed along to the U.S. government as a labor cost. To the extent that pension expense increases, pension cost (labor cost) increases. That cost can be passed along through a defense contract to the federal government, who then passes the increased pension cost to the taxpayer through a tax increase. Defense contractors and utilities (a regulated industry) are in a unique position when it comes to pension cost.

Question: Should we consider using a variable for valuation that excludes pensions, such as earnings before interest, taxes, depreciation, amortization, and pension (EBITDAP)?

Zion: I wouldn't take all pension-related items out of the analysis. I would leave in service cost because it is a real compensation cost, albeit a deferred compensation cost. It is the present value of the future retirement benefits that employees have earned by working during the current year. But I would agree that you could get rid of all pension cost components, except for service cost.

Question: What are the most common smoothing mechanisms in accounting for pension cost?

Zion: A lot of smoothing mechanisms exist. One involves the expected return on plan assets (the amount, not the rate). Companies use an expected rate of return—10 percent, 9 percent, 12 percent, whatever. But what do they multiply this expected return rate by? Although some companies multiply it by the fair value of the pension assets, some companies do not. Some companies take that expected rate of return and multiply it by what the accountants refer to as a "calculated value"—the market-related value of plan assets, not the market value, which means that you take the expected rate of return and multiply it by, say, a five-year moving average of the pension assets. This smoothing mechanism is important. In 2001, pension plan assets declined, but the expected return went higher for some companies—not the rate but the actual dollar amount. How did that happen? The increase was a result of this smoothing mechanism that is built into pension accounting.

Another important smoothing mechanism surrounds unrecognized gains and losses. Companies record an expected return on their plan assets. But what happens once the actual return is known? The difference between the actual and expected return is pushed off the balance sheet. If the actual return is less than the expected return, it is an unrecognized loss. If the actual return is more than the expected return, it is an unrecognized gain. Those gains and losses accumulate over time and eventually are recognized.

Question: How frequently do companies modify their expected return assumptions?

Zion: If a company is continually changing its pension asset allocation, the expected return would probably change frequently. But if a company maintains a set mix of pension assets, the expected return shouldn't change very often unless the company's view of the future return on those assets changes.

I have found that for most companies the expected return doesn't change often. For S&P 500 companies, for example, the median expected return from 1991 to 1997 was 9 percent; from 1998 to 2001, it subsequently rose to 9.2 percent and has been 9.2 percent ever since. So, in that large group of companies over that 10-year period, some companies have changed their expected return, but certainly others have not.

Question: What adjustments can an analyst make if a company has obviously absurd assumptions?

Zion: Expected return is easy to adjust. For example, if a company has an expected return assumption of 10 percent and you believe it should be 5 percent, take the difference between the two and multiply the market value of pension asset by that difference. This will give you the impact on earnings for the next year. Your earnings estimate for the next year can then be reduced by this amount.

The discount rate is more difficult to adjust. For accounting purposes, a company has to use the yield on high-grade corporate bonds as the discount rate. Since the early 1990s, when the U.S. SEC named Moody's AA index as a good example of a high-grade index to be used for discount rate purposes, it has been the gold standard for most companies. First, you have to decide if the high-grade yield makes sense as the discount rate. Second, compare any recent changes in the market yield with changes made by the company in its discount rate. For example, in 2001, yields in the market fell, but a number of companies raised their discount rate. That may make sense given a company's particular circumstances, but then again it may not. Discount rates vary from country to country. And discount rates vary based on the age of a company's workforce. For example, a company with a younger workforce has a longer-term obligation, which requires a different discount rate from a company with an older workforce. A quick back-of-the-envelope calculation will show that for each 100-bp change in the discount rate, assuming a 10-year duration, the pension obligation will move by about 10 percent.

In our report, we made a model available for evaluating individual company information. The model can be found at www.csfb.com/equity/presentations/pension_forecast_model.xls. So, you can plug in the information from a pension footnote along with your own set of assumptions, and the model will forecast the pension cost, the obligation, the funded status, funding requirements, and so on.

Question: How are the other postretirement benefits accounted for?

Zion: The accounting for other postretirement benefits is covered in SFAS No. 106, which is very similar to SFAS No. 87. The footnotes for the pension plan and for the other postretirement benefits look exactly the same because the accounting is quite similar. The economics, however, are different because the other postretirement benefits generally aren't funded. They fall under the "pay-as-you-go" category.

Why aren't they funded? First, because companies don't get a tax advantage when they fund postretirement benefits, and second, because companies simply aren't required to fund them. There's no ERISA-type law for the other postretirement benefits.

The cost of other postretirement benefits reflected on the income statement is typically close to their actual cash cost; although not exact, it's in the ballpark. And the postretirement benefit obligation shown on the balance sheet is also typically more accurate than the pension obligation. This is because the other postretirement benefits generally involve no assets and thus no smoothing mechanisms. Therefore, the financial statements provide a better picture of the true cost of the other postretirement benefits than they do of the pension benefit.

Question: To what extent has the market reacted to the heightened concern about pension obligations?

Zion: That concern is being factored in by the market, but how much is hard to say. For some companies, the market may be overcompensating—as if it is facing the worst-case scenario—for worries about the pension obligation.

A lot of investors have been asking for our report, which leads me to believe that the market still needs to make sense of pension accounting, funding requirements, and their impact on the balance sheet. I think many investors view the pension plan as a black hole.

I recall one particular meeting in which we were discussing the details of pension accounting and someone asked, "Is this so complicated that I should just ignore it?" That's not the right attitude, but some investors think that way. Everyone is still trying to get comfortable with pension accounting, but it will take some time.

Accounting (or Not) for Employee Stock Options

Jane B. Adams
Managing Director
Maverick Capital, Ltd.
New York City

> Accounting for employee stock options (ESOs) remains a controversial subject because current accounting and reporting methods are deficient. Recent abuses by certain executives have led to heightened scrutiny of how companies treat ESOs. More important, the increased attention may provide the impetus necessary to improve the financial reporting for this form of compensation, and some reforms are already taking shape.

Most investment professionals agree (at least conceptually) that employee stock options (ESOs) are a form of compensation whose expense should be included in the income statement, although measuring their value continues to be debated. I urge investment professionals to actively support the standard-setting processes of the International Accounting Standards Board (IASB) and the Financial Accounting Standards Board (FASB), which aim to enhance the information investors are provided about ESOs. The IASB, in particular, has embraced the notion that investment professionals should not have to dig through the notes of financial statements to find operating expenses.

In this presentation, I will identify the accounting methods used by companies for measuring ESOs and the information that is provided about employee stock compensation plans in financial statements. Additionally, I dispute corporate arguments against expensing the fair value of ESOs. Also, some companies have announced an intent to begin expensing the fair value of ESOs, and investors should understand the different ways in which companies that adopt fair value expensing for ESO plans may be reporting the expense in their financial statements.

The Measurement Debate

Until 2002, only 7 companies (only 2 in the S&P 500 Index) reported ESO expense at fair value, but as of October 2002, 118 companies have announced their intent to adopt the fair value method of expensing ESOs. Because of the large number of companies announcing their intent to change their accounting policy for ESOs—both the *Wall Street Journal* and Standard & Poor's (S&P) are maintaining lists of companies electing to report ESO expense at fair value—the FASB has proposed several ways those changes can be reflected in financial statements.[1] And the IASB has published an exposure draft on ESO expensing that will spur discussions of the various valuation methods.[2]

Calculation of Option Value. Public companies can choose between two methods for valuing their options' expense: fair value or intrinsic value. Depending on the measurement method selected, companies will measure the awards on the grant date or when the terms of the awards become fixed (which in many cases is the grant date).

■ *Valuation method.* Of the two valuation methods for public companies—fair value and intrinsic value—most companies in the United States use the intrinsic value method. Under the intrinsic value method that is outlined in Accounting Principles

---

[1] A final statement (SFAS No. 148, *Accounting for Stock-Based Compensation—Transition and Disclosure*) was published by the FASB in December 2002.

[2] The IASB issued ED 2, *Share-Based Payment*, on 7 November 2002. A copy can be downloaded at www.iasb.org.uk/docs/ed02/ed02.pdf.

Board (APB) Opinion No. 25, if a company fixes the option's exercise (or strike) price at the prevailing market price on the date of grant and fixes the number of shares to which an employee is entitled, no expense is required to be recognized for the option issuance because the intrinsic value is zero. The intrinsic value method, unlike the fair value method that I will discuss shortly, ignores the time value, as well as the volatility, of the options and thus undervalues the true upside of the options' value to the recipient and the true compensation expense to the issuing company. Nevertheless, despite these deficiencies (or, more likely, because of these deficiencies), most U.S. companies have fixed ESO plans and use the intrinsic value method for valuing ESOs.

If, however, the strike price or the number of shares to which the employee is entitled can vary at the date of grant, the ESO plan is a variable plan. APB No. 25 provides that a company with a variable plan must remeasure compensation expense in the amount of the difference between the market price and the exercise or strike price in each period until the exercise price and the number of shares become fixed. This remeasurement is done by estimating during interim periods (prior to the terms of the grant becoming fixed) the number of shares and strike price and adjusting compensation expense for any increase or decrease in the intrinsic value based on updated interim estimates.

A second valuation alternative, the fair value method, was introduced as the preferred method with the release of the FASB's Statement of Financial Accounting Standards (SFAS) No. 123, *Accounting for Stock-Based Compensation*, in 1995.[3] SFAS No. 123 provides rules for estimating the fair value of ESOs using an option-pricing model, such as a Black–Scholes or binomial model. SFAS No. 123 allows companies to choose between the intrinsic value and fair value methods. As a consequence, SFAS No. 123 allows—but does not require—the compensation cost resulting from the granting of stock options to employees to be measured at fair value and reported in the income statement over the period in which the options vest. Companies that elect the intrinsic value measurement method, however, must disclose, on a pro forma basis, the fair value ESO expense. (SFAS No. 123 provides for the use of a third valuation method—the minimum value method—for nonpublic companies only. Although it uses the same inputs as the fair value option-pricing model, it assumes a volatility of zero, and volatility, which captures the potential to participate in a wide range of upside results, is a key driver in an option's value.

[3] For a summary of SFAS No. 123, please see Appendix B.

Thus, the minimum value method is guaranteed to produce an incorrect valuation.)

Inputs to the option-pricing models used to calculate the fair value of ESOs include the following:
- exercise (strike) price,
- current price of the underlying stock,
- expected volatility (historical, average, annualized volatility over the period commensurate with the options' expected life, adjusted for expectations that differ from past experience),
- expected dividend yield,
- expected term of the option, and
- risk-free interest rate during the expected term.

At the end of 2001, 498 of the companies in the S&P 500 used the intrinsic value method with footnote disclosures. Yet, even though the disclosed numbers do not affect earnings, a bias toward understating the pro forma ESO compensation expense still appears to exist.

■ *Measurement dates.* The measurement date—grant date, vesting date, or exercise date—is important because it reflects when the remeasurement of the options' value stops being recorded in the financial statements. For example, as we have seen over the past several years, an option's value can vary significantly over time. If the expense of a stock option grant is determined only at the date of grant, subsequent changes in value would not be captured. If the award's fair value continues to be remeasured through a later date—vesting or exercise—expense would be adjusted to reflect the revised values. Although many analysts agree that the value of the option at grant date is an appropriate measure of the compensation expense that should be recorded, some analysts would prefer recording the change in an option's value subsequent to grant date as a financing expense because the employee does not have to "pay" up front—that is, at grant date—for the award. Some analysts view the change in the option value subsequent to vesting to be a holding gain or loss from stock price change, which they would record not as a component of compensation but as a change in value that should be recognized in order to record the ultimate issuance of the stock at its fair value when (and if) issued. Therefore, the amount expensed for ESO compensation cost or financing cost will depend on the method and date required for a company to account for its ESO plan.

The IASB has chosen a grant date model for measuring stock option expense. The FASB uses a "modified" grant date model.

■ *Option-pricing model adjustments.* The FASB and the IASB have stated that adjustments should be made to the option-pricing model when it is used to measure ESOs—adjustments that are not made when measuring exchange-traded options. A primary difference is an adjustment to reflect the nontransferability of ESOs. Once stock options vest, employees have no way to extract or monetize the value of that option except by exercising the option (i.e., the ESOs typically cannot be transferred or sold to another party). To reflect the fact that most ESOs are exercised earlier than the expiration of the contract (thus leaving time value on the table), the FASB and the IASB use an expected life of the option as the model input rather than its contract life. (An option's expected life is how long the option is likely to be held before exercise, not how long it can be held.) The shorter the expected life a company adopts, the lower the fair value will be for that option grant and thus the lower the compensation expense that has to be disclosed (or recognized for those companies that are expensing the fair value of option grants). Academic research has identified a bias on the part of companies—in particular, those companies that are heavy users of ESOs—to choose a shorter expected life in valuing ESOs.

Adjustments are also required to reflect that the options could be forfeited (i.e., could fail to vest) during the vesting period. If an employee leaves a job prior to being vested, that employee's stock options are forfeited. SFAS No. 123 captures the possible diminution in value by virtue of forfeiture by requiring companies to adjust ESO expense as forfeitures occur or to make an assumption at the outset by estimating how many of the options are expected to vest. Then, periodically, the company will "true up" the expense to reflect the actual amount of experienced forfeitures that differed from the amount that was assumed.

Differences between the IASB and the FASB.

On several issues, the approach taken by the IASB has differed slightly from that of the FASB, as is evident in the IASB exposure draft. For example, to account for the possibility of forfeiture during the vesting period, the IASB requires companies to estimate at grant date the decrement in fair value as a result of the risk of forfeiting the grant during the vesting period. The reasoning is that a grant that is subject to forfeiture has less value than a grant that is vested. The value of the option grant is not changed if the subsequent trend in forfeitures changes. As I just described, under the FASB's modified grant date model (SFAS No. 123), compensation expense would not be recorded for option awards that fail to vest.

Consistent with current U.S. GAAP, the IASB's exposure draft proposes that ESOs be valued on the date they are granted (not on the date they vest, as had been originally planned), and consistent with SFAS No. 123, it proposes that in the absence of market prices, companies calculate option value using an option-pricing model, such as a Black–Scholes or binomial model. The IASB's exposure draft also articulates the objective of the measurement of stock options awarded to employees as being at fair value, the same as options that would be awarded to nonemployees.

The IASB, however, is taking a slightly different route from the FASB in its approach to measuring the value of an equity award for a nonpublic company. It reasons that whether a company is public or nonpublic, the objective is to measure the fair value of the award. Whereas the FASB allows nonpublic companies to use the minimum value method and thus ignore volatility, the IASB does not provide any exceptions for nonpublic companies and requires that nonpublic companies estimate the effects of volatility on the value of the award. Holders of ESOs, whether public or nonpublic, benefit from the right to participate in increases in the share price over an option's life while not having to bear the full risk of loss from decreases in the share price.

Pro Forma Disclosures

When valuing a company, analysts should scrutinize a company's ESO disclosures. Despite the shortcomings of the current system, companies are required to provide a great deal of information in the notes of their financial statements, as well as meaningful incremental information in their proxy statements.

What to Look For. To assess aspects of a company's ESO plan, including the potential impact on the company's bottom line, analysts should look for the following disclosures in the notes of a company's financial statements: options granted, options exercised, options forfeited, weighted-average strike prices, fair value of options granted, assumptions used, fair value expense and/or pro forma net income, and the EPS impact. Incremental information is also often provided in proxy statements.

In performing comparative analyses of companies, the answers to the following questions can be significant:

- What is the rate of grant? Has it been changing? A recent study by Pearl Meyer indicated that "The Top 200 companies reported a fifth straight year of dramatic growth in the rate at which they grant shares to management and employees increasing 17% over last year [2000] to 2.69% of weighted average shares outstanding. Overall, the 'burn rate' increased more than 2.5 times in

the past decade and about 80% in the last five years."[4]
- If the company has a nonqualified ESO plan, what is the size of the tax benefit?
- How will options granted, or that are available for grant but that have not yet been granted, affect dilution? Pearl Meyer also noted, "A record 16.23 percent of shares outstanding has been set aside for management and employee equity incentives by the Top 200 companies. This represents almost a doubling over the last 10 years and about a 40% increase in five years."[5]
- What is the per-employee fair value expense?
- What percentage of options granted are to the top five executives identified in the proxy?
- How does equity compensation affect cash compensation?

In some cases, the direct link between equity and cash compensation is obvious. The Rite Aid Corporation recently was able to negotiate with its employees to reduce the portion of cash compensation in exchange for increasing the portion of stock (or ESO) compensation. Clearly, analysts can benefit from asking these types of questions.

New proxy rules required by the U.S. SEC effective in the spring of 2002 require companies to disclose information about ESO plans that have been voted on by shareholders and those that have not. This information can yield interesting insights into the corporate governance attitude of management. The NYSE and National Association of Securities Dealers' listing proposals would require all ESO plans to be approved by shareholders.

Microsoft Corporation's Disclosures. Microsoft's 10-K notes provide insight into the amount of information that can be gleaned from the footnotes to a company's financial statements. **Table 1** shows that Microsoft made a large number of ESO grants in 2000 and 2001. One reason for the higher number of options granted is that instead of repricing underwater options, Microsoft issued new ESOs at lower strike prices, without rescinding prior grants. I included the column "vesting period" to emphasize that whether a company makes only pro forma disclosures or is one of the 118 companies embracing higher-quality financial reporting by recognizing the fair value of its ESO expense on its income statement, the expense is attributed to the employee services received during the vesting period. (Different plans use different vesting formulas. Our assumption is for a cliff-vesting plan.[6]) **Table 2** illustrates the potential dilution from Microsoft's grants.

Tax Benefit. The tax benefits to employers from ESO compensation should not be overlooked. The tax laws distinguish between nonqualified ESOs and incentive stock options. Upon an employee's exercise of a nonqualified ESO, the company receives a tax deduction for compensation expense equal to the intrinsic value of the option upon exercise. (The employee reports compensation income in that amount too.) SFAS No. 123 states, however, that no tax benefit can appear in the income statement unless compensation expense has also been recorded in the income statement. A company using the intrinsic value method, which typically results in zero compensation expense being recognized in the income statement (because grants are typically fixed awards with an exercise price in excess of the market price on the date of grant), reports the tax benefit received in its cash flow statement, in its reconciliation of shareholder equity, or in the footnotes to its financial statements, but not in its income statement. The employee is taxed at exercise (regardless of whether the stock is immediately liquidated).

---

[4]"2001 Equity Stake: Study of Management Equity Participation in the Top 200 Corporations," Pearl Meyer & Partners (2002):8–9.
[5]Ibid., 6.

[6]A cliff-vesting plan vests 100 percent of the award after completion of the required period of service, say four years. The expense would be recognized ratably (straightline) over that four-year period.

Table 1. Microsoft's Grant Activity

Year	FV/Option	Number of Options Granted (millions)	Total (A) (millions)	Vesting Period (B)	Ratable (A/B) (millions)
1998	$11.81	138	1,630	4.5 years	362.2
1999	20.90	78	1,630	4.5	362.3
2000	36.67	304	11,147	4.5	2,477.11
2001	29.31	224	6,565	4.5	1,459.0
2002	31.57	41	1,294	4.5	287.6

Note: FV = fair value.

Table 2. Microsoft's Potential Dilution

Year	Number of Options Granted (millions)	Total Grants Outstanding (millions)	Shares Outstanding (millions)	Potential Dilution from Annual Grants	Potential Dilution from All Grants
1998	138	893	4,864	2.8%	18.5%
1999	78	766	5,028	1.6	15.2
2000	304	832	5,189	5.9	16.0
2001	224	898	5,341	4.2	16.8
2002	41	802	5,406	0.8	14.8

The tax benefit from ESOs can be significant. In 2000, the tax benefit for companies in the S&P 500 was about $3,000 per employee. **Table 3** shows Microsoft's tax benefit from its ESOs for the past five years. It also is important to evaluate the effect of this tax benefit on cash flow from operations (CFFO). An analyst may want to back out this number because it is not within the company's control; the tax benefit occurs only when an employee elects to exercise.

Shortcomings. Current financial reporting based on the intrinsic value, disclosure-only standard is deficient. The vast majority of financial statements do not reflect the full consequences of ESO transactions. As a result, operating costs are understated and profits and shareholder value are overstated. Current accounting practice leads investors to believe that options have a zero value, but clearly, this is not true.

Consider the pro forma impact on EPS. Had ESOs been measured at fair value and expensed in income statements, the aggregate, diluted EPS for companies in the S&P 500 would have declined by 8 percent in 2000 and 20 percent in 2001.[7] Microsoft provides us with additional data that allow analysts to put the size of this expense in context by measuring the pro forma impact of ESOs on operating income, which is helpful because analysts typically do not have the information to adjust the pro forma net income effect for any tax benefits assumed in that calculation.

Corporate Argument Against Expensing

Warren Buffett's criticism of the current rules for accounting for ESOs rings true for many: "If options aren't compensation, what are they? If compensation isn't an operating expense, what is it? And if expenses shouldn't go into the calculation of earnings, where in the world should they go?"[8] Although the corporate argument against expensing options has evolved over the years, it still lacks substance.

At first, the corporate argument against measuring and expensing the fair value of option grants was that stock options are not a compensation expense of the company but are a grant by the shareholders to employees. If nonemployees had rendered the service in exchange for the option grants, however, the grant would have been an expense. What is the logic behind the two situations being treated differently? And when equity is used to acquire another company, the fair value of the equity is used to measure the value of the net assets acquired. Again, what is the logic behind treating these two types of equity issuance differently?

The next corporate argument against expensing was that it would result in double counting: Expensing options affects both the numerator and the denominator in the EPS calculation. But if equity options were granted in exchange for advertising services, advertising expense would be reported and the shares outstanding would be adjusted. Again, why should there be a difference?

---

[7] Pat McConnell and Janet Pegg, "Employee Stock Option Expense: Is the Time Right for Change?" Bear Stearns (July 2002).

[8] Warren E. Buffett, "Chairman's Letter," *1998 Annual Report*, Berkshire Hathaway, Inc.

Table 3. Microsoft's Tax Benefit, 1998–2002

Year	Tax Benefit ($ millions)	CFFO ($ millions)	Number of Employees	Tax Benefit/ CFFO	Tax Benefit/ Employee
1998	1,553	8,433	27,055	18.4%	$ 57,402
1999	3,107	13,137	31,396	23.7	98,962
2000	5,535	11,426	39,100	48.4	141,560
2001	2,066	13,422	47,600	15.4	43,403
2002	1,596	14,509	50,500	11.0	31,604

Clearly, the issuance of options can have a significant dilutive effect on EPS. In 2001, 64 companies in the S&P 500 issued ESOs that exceeded 5 percent of their shares outstanding. For each year from 1999 through 2001, the number of such companies ranged between 59 and 77. And 26 companies granted ESOs to their employees equal to more than 5 percent of shares outstanding in *each* of those three years. Not only is the issuance of options occurring at significant percentages of a company's outstanding shares, the number outstanding at any given time can be significant: 33 companies in the S&P 500 have options outstanding in excess of 20 percent of their total shares outstanding. The impact of these awards on compensation and on dilution should not be ignored by valuation models.

Today, the main argument against expensing is that options cannot be valued with sufficient reliability to record them as an expense in a company's income statement. This argument is dubious on a number of fronts.

Although subjective judgment does come into play, financial statements include many items based on estimates and subjective judgments. A similar argument was made concerning retiree health care benefits, which were required to be measured and recorded as part of compensation expense beginning in 1993. The push to measure and reflect as an expense the value of the benefits promised has provided better information to investors and to management and has resulted in higher-quality financial reporting. Another measurement that has been demonstrated to be highly subjective is the reporting of restructuring charges. The FASB's Emerging Issues Task Force model (Issue 94-3, *Liability Recognition for Certain Employee Termination Benefits and Other Costs to Exit an Activity* [*Including Certain Costs Incurred in a Restructuring*]), which I view as elective, clearly has caused amounts subject to large measurement error to be recorded as expense in one period only to be reversed in subsequent reporting periods. Option-pricing models have been used and refined for the past three decades. Although some input adjustments may be necessary to estimate the fair value of a company's ESOs, the fact that adjustments are necessary does not obviate the power of the tools available or the relevance of the estimate.

Another problem with maintaining the status quo (permitting the use of intrinsic value to measure ESO expense) is that it motivates companies to use fixed plans (i.e., fixed strike prices and a fixed number of awards) to achieve a grant-date intrinsic value of zero and discourages the use of performance-based plans. The accounting results in an illogical outcome in that fixed plans, which are typically viewed as more valuable, result in zero expense being reported in the income statement, whereas performance-based plans (variable plans) result in an expense being recorded each period until the grant terms are fixed. Thus, the variable plans look as though they are more expensive, and investors are led to believe that the fixed awards have no cost.

The inadequacy of the corporate argument is intensified by the fact that material information is missing from financial statements. During the 1990s, the use of ESO programs increased markedly, with the number of shares granted annually more than doubling. Among the 200 largest public companies, ESOs totaling more than 2.6 percent of shares outstanding have been awarded to employees in exchange for service, but according to the financial statements of the issuing companies, the value of these grants has been zero. This annual rate of grant more than doubled during the 1990s.

An AIMR member survey challenges the corporate lobby that claims investors do not use the information on ESOs and that the information would simply be backed out of the income statement if it were incorporated. In a September 2001 AIMR member survey, 81 percent of the respondents said that they use information about stock options when evaluating a company's performance and determining its value, and 66 percent said they use the information regardless of where that information is found. Only 19 percent said they do not use the information at all. In addition, 74 percent answered "yes" when asked, "Do the current accounting requirements for share-based payments need improving, in particular, for those plans covering employees?" Eighty-three percent of respondents said that the accounting method for all payment transactions in shares (including those given in ESO plans) should require recognition of an expense in the income statement, and 88 percent said they consider share-based or stock option plans to be compensation to the parties receiving the benefits.

Need for Vigilance

The increased use of ESOs requires that managements and boards of directors wisely exercise their fiduciary responsibility in accounting and reporting. If options are a good idea, then providing additional information about the economic consequences of their grant should not change that fact. Neutral, unbiased accounting can only help investors and shareholders. Good disclosure neither compensates nor is an adequate substitute for accounting. Investors should not have to dig through the footnotes to find operating costs. The following steps are paramount:

raising investor awareness about these issues, being vigilant in exposing corporate abuses of the system, and supporting the accounting standard setters who are working to improve the accounting for these awards.

Biases. As I mentioned earlier, biases can be observed in the measurement of ESO value. Bias most commonly appears in the assumptions about the expected life of a company's outstanding ESOs and volatility. Consider the following example that illustrates the sensitivity of the measurement to the assumptions used: Siebel Systems offered $1.85 for each option held by its employees that had a strike price greater than $40. (The share price at the time of offer was $8.60.) Graef Crystal, a well-known compensation expert, estimated that Siebel used a 3.4-year expected life to value the option.[9] If an 8-year expected life had been used, the option's value would have been $3.22. He also estimated that a volatility assumption of 70 percent had been used. Mr. Crystal observed that if the top 1 percent of "way-out" scenarios were excluded, the value of the grant would drop from $3.22 to $1.02. Clearly, disclosures of all the valuation assumptions made by a company can help analysts detect bias. In a Bear Stearns analysis of the volatility assumptions used by companies in 2000 and 2001, 331 of 489 companies increased their volatility assumptions year over year, 94 reduced them, and 64 left them unchanged.[10] The idea that companies would have expected lower volatility in 2001 than in 2000 seems incredible.

Incorporating Options into Valuation. The granting of ESOs can be viewed as the culmination of two transactions: a financing cash inflow (raising cash by issuing equity into the markets) and an operating cash outflow (paying that cash to employees in exchange for services rendered). If ESOs were not used as employee compensation, cash would be used. So, the argument "it is not cash, so back it out of expense and ignore it" is without merit. ESOs are an operating expense that companies have to incur in one form or another.

In addition, looking at data from 2000, we found that 68 percent of the companies with option programs in 2000 also repurchased shares and used 48 percent of their net income to do so. Clearly, the use of ESOs affects the choices that management makes about its use of cash.

---

[9] Graef Crystal is a full-time columnist and editor-at-large at *Bloomberg News*.

[10] Pat McConnell and Janet Pegg, "Employee Stock Option Expense: Is the Time Right for Change?" Bear Stearns (July 2002).

S&P's "core earnings" measures, which will be incorporating the fair value of option grants into the S&P measures of index performance, are an effort to make earnings measures comparable among different companies and should be commended. S&P's core earnings will be benefited by the new FASB standard (Statement 148, issued in December 2002) that requires companies to provide pro forma information about ESO expense on a quarterly basis.

Option Repricing. Investors should also beware of option-repricing events, which may not be in the best interest of investors. A recent FASB Interpretation (FASB Interpretation No. 44) requires that repriced ESOs be treated as if they were issued under a variable plan, so that going forward, compensation expense would be recorded based on the intrinsic value of the repriced ESOs until they were exercised.

But a practice has evolved that seems to have as its objective circumventing the requirements of Interpretation 44. Interpretation 44 views any option issuance and option rescission that occur (in any order) within a six-month period to be an option repricing. To circumvent this rule, companies have used a "six-and-one" repricing, in which a company offers to cancel outstanding ESOs and reissue them at the market price on the date of reissuance six months and one day after cancellation. This practice has avoided repricing consequences (keeping ESO-related compensation expense from affecting the income statement). Of greater concern is that during the six-month period, employees and shareholders are in diametrically opposed positions because employees are motivated to have the lowest share price possible when their options are repriced in six months and one day.

FASB Transition Methods. The FASB has recently issued Statement 148, which amends how companies that are just now moving to fair value measurements of options expense should reflect that transition in the financial statements. When SFAS No. 123 was issued in 1995, it presumed that companies transitioning to a fair value method would not have any of the historical data that we have had now for seven years. Consequently, Statement 123 required prospective application of fair value (i.e., fair value expense for option grants occurring after the date of adoption, which causes expense to rise over the vesting period for each subsequent grant). Given that companies have been measuring this expense since 1995, the FASB has indicated that two additional methods of transitioning can be chosen. The prospective method, which recognizes the fair value of option grants made after adoption of the fair value method, may be adopted now but will not be permitted for changes made after December 2003. The second transition method records expense in the current and prospective period for all awards not yet vested, beginning in the year that the fair value method is adopted. The third alternative is to restate all financial statements as though fair value had been used for all ESOs granted, modified, or settled in fiscal years beginning after 15 December 1994. Analysts should keep in mind that given these different choices, companies' financial statements may not be comparable. To compensate for this potential lack of comparability, Statement 148 specifies expanded disclosures requiring comparable information for all companies, regardless of whether, when, or how a company adopts the preferred fair value method of accounting for ESOs.

Conclusion

The battle over accounting for ESOs rages on because the status quo accounting and reporting methods are deficient. Although much of today's focus on ESO accounting stems from boom-time abuses by some executives, who allocated themselves large stock grants, exercised them, and then sold them for huge gains, the heightened attention will, I hope, provide the impetus for change that not only exposes the abuses but improves the financial reporting of this form of compensation for all companies and all investors. Until then, investors and potential investors will bear the price of the deficient accounting.

With so many important changes on the horizon in the world of accounting for ESOs—including the IASB's exposure draft and the FASB's efforts to bring about international convergence—a great opportunity exists for investors to make a difference. I encourage investment professionals to participate in the debate by supporting the IASB's exposure draft, which proposes recognizing ESO expense at fair value. The FASB should be encouraged to modify its standards to require the expensing of all stock options at fair value. Until the requirements are changed, investors should encourage companies to adopt voluntarily the measurement and expensing of ESOs at fair value.

Accounting and Reporting for Derivatives and Hedging Transactions

Donald J. Smith
*Associate Professor of Finance and Faculty Director, M.B.A. Program
School of Management, Boston University
Boston*

> Corporate use of derivatives (and occasional misuses) created quite a stir in the 1990s, prompting the Financial Accounting Standards Board (FASB) to issue Statement of Financial Accounting Standard (SFAS) No. 133. What differentiates SFAS No. 133 from previous FASB guidelines is its definition of a derivative and an embedded derivative and its treatment of fair value hedges, cash flow hedges, and exchange rate or investment in foreign operations hedges.

In the 1980s, the Financial Accounting Standards Board (FASB) recognized the need for a complete and consistent set of guidelines for the accounting and reporting of derivatives and hedging transactions. Statement of Financial Accounting Standards (SFAS) No. 52, SFAS No. 80, and various FASB Emerging Issues Task Force publications addressed the accounting and reporting of several specific types of derivatives, but along the lines of accounting for forward contracts applied to currency risk management or futures applied to commodity price or interest rate risk management. That is, the accounting rules were written on a product-by-product basis and prescribed different guidance for economically equivalent positions. Thus, steps had to be taken to harmonize the accounting for derivatives.

Perhaps more than anything else, the abuses in the 1990s spurred the FASB to address the issue and to release SFAS No. 133. One of the landmark events in the world of derivatives abuses in the 1990s was the case involving Procter & Gamble (P&G). Because the P&G story is an excellent illustration of the problems posed by derivatives and how such events changed the industry's accounting for and reporting of derivatives, I will discuss this story in some detail. The postscript to this story is positive because senior management at P&G used this particular event to reform and update policies for risk assessment and now embraces state-of-the-art methodologies, such as value at risk.

I will then discuss three types of risk associated with derivatives hedging—exposure to changes in the fair value of assets or liabilities, exposure to changes in the cash flows of assets or liabilities, and exposure to foreign exchange rates and net investment in foreign operations—and how they are addressed under SFAS No. 133. As part of this discussion, I will define the characteristics of a derivative and an embedded derivative under SFAS No. 133. I will conclude with several observations on SFAS No. 133 and its implications for financial analysis.[1]

P&G's Infamous Swap

The P&G story starts in the summer of 1993, when interest rates were very low, the yield curve was very steep, and a lot of investment strategies were based on the steep yield curve. P&G had entered into several receive-fixed (and pay floating) interest rate swaps with Bankers Trust (BT). As interest rates in general came down and the yield curve steepened, those

---

Editor's Note: For further discussion concerning some of the topics addressed in this presentation, see Christopher L. Culp, Merton H. Miller, and Andres M.P. Neves, "Value at Risk: Uses and Abuses," *Journal of Applied Corporate Finance* (Winter 1998):26–38. This article is available at aimrpubs.org in the "2003 CFA Curriculum: Refresher Readings for Charterholders" section: www.aimr.org/memservices/private/pdf/pubs/ValueatRisk.pdf.

[1] For more information on SFAS No. 133, see Gary L. Gastineau, Donald J. Smith, and Rebecca Todd, CFA, *Risk Management, Derivatives, and Financial Analysis under SFAS No. 133* (Charlottesville, VA: The Research Foundation of AIMR, 2001). For a summary of SFAS No. 133, please see Appendix C.

swaps did well. P&G then gave BT an aggressive target for future swaps. That target was a funding rate equal to the commercial paper (CP) rate less 40 bps. Given that the difference at the time between CP and T-bill yields was about 25 bps, P&G was asking for a sub-Treasury cost of funds, an aggressive move by any measure. P&G wanted a transaction size of $100 million for a five-year period. At the time, BT was showing many of its customers a strategy called either the "5/30" or "2/30" deal, which involved two points along the Treasury yield curve. The two points were the 5-year (or 2-year) Treasury yield and the 30-year Treasury yield. In effect, the strategy was a bet on interest rate stability. The deal that BT showed P&G could have potentially delivered a funding rate to P&G of CP less 75 bps, much better than P&G's target. P&G took the deal in November 1993 and doubled the target transaction size to $200 million.

Swap Specifics. A common strategy for using an interest rate swap is for a company that has issued fixed-rate debt to swap the fixed interest payment for a lower, floating-rate (or variable) interest payment. In 1993, a reasonable fixed rate to pay for financing in the intermediate-term debt market for a company of P&G's credit standing was about 5.3 percent, which is the rate I will use to illustrate the strategy. The transaction that BT proposed had P&G receiving a fixed rate of 5.3 percent (effectively offsetting its interest payment obligation on its outstanding debt) and paying CP semiannually for five years. Most interest rate swaps are based on a single, periodic observation of three-month LIBOR, but the swap BT proposed to P&G was based on the daily observations of the 30-day CP rate, averaged over a six-month time period, minus 75 bps plus an amount named "spread." Spread was set at zero for the first six months of the swap, which meant that P&G would pay CP minus 75 bps for the first six months of the swap—an unbelievably low funding cost.

Spread was defined by a formula that would be calculated once in May 1994 and used for the remaining 4.5 years of the swap. The famous, "brain-twisting" formula for spread is

$$\text{Spread} = \max\left[0, \frac{\left(98.5 \times \frac{5\text{-Year CMT}}{5.78}\right) - (30\text{-Year Treasury Price})}{100}\right]$$

where CMT equals the constant maturity Treasury yield (published by the U.S. Federal Reserve Bank) and the 30-year Treasury price equals the price of the most recent on-the-run 30-year Treasury bond quoted flat (without accrued interest).

With the swap having begun in November 1993, the terms for the remaining life of the swap were to be based on observations of the 5-year Treasury yield and the 30-year Treasury price in May 1994 (the end of the first six months of the swap). If the result from the formula was zero or negative, then P&G's cost of funds on the $200 million liability would be CP minus 75 bps for the entire five-year life of the swap. If the result was positive, then spread would chew into the 75 bps subtracted from CP, thus raising the interest rate paid by P&G.

Swap Rationale. When the story hit the press in 1994, the swap was described as being incredibly complex. Ironically, the risk analysis for the swap was only a spreadsheet away, or perhaps more accurately, only a term-structure model away. By substituting various values in the formula, the possible values for spread could easily have been calculated. The risk analysis was simply an assessment of how interest rates were likely to change from November 1993 to May 1994. Spread would be positive if the 5-year Treasury yield rose and/or if the 30-year Treasury yield rose, causing the price of the 30-year Treasury price to fall. So, the bet was on two points on the yield curve—the 5- and 30-year points—and their relationship to each other; essentially, the bet was on the shape of the yield curve.

P&G entered the swap hoping to receive an extremely inexpensive funding cost—75 bps less than CP. On the $200 million notional principal, the total potential benefit to P&G was about $6.5 million in present-value terms. The risk was that yields would rise over the first six months of the swap. This swap structure had the same effect as writing put options on Treasuries. When an investor buys a put option on a T-bond, the value of the put increases as the bond price falls and the yield rises. Alternatively, if the investor writes a put, the investor collects the premium paid for the put but stands to lose if the bond price falls and the yield rises. P&G implicitly wrote put options on two points on the Treasury yield curve.

Swap Results. Figure 1 shows the changes in the 5- and 30-year Treasury yields from October 1992 to November 1993. The yields were fairly stable, falling only slightly, with a relatively significant spread between the two during this period. **Figure 2** shows the changes in the 5-year and 30-year Treasury yields from November 1993 to May 1994, during the first six months of the swap. Rates rose, causing the swap to move against P&G. No calamity had caused rates to rise; they rose merely as a result of a normal Federal Reserve (Fed) tightening operation. And with higher rates, market volatility moved higher as well. P&G lost money not because rates reacted bizarrely or atypically to an unusual event but because rates simply trended higher as part of a normal, cyclical pattern.

Figure 1. Five-Year and Thirty-Year Treasury Yields, October 1992 to November 1993

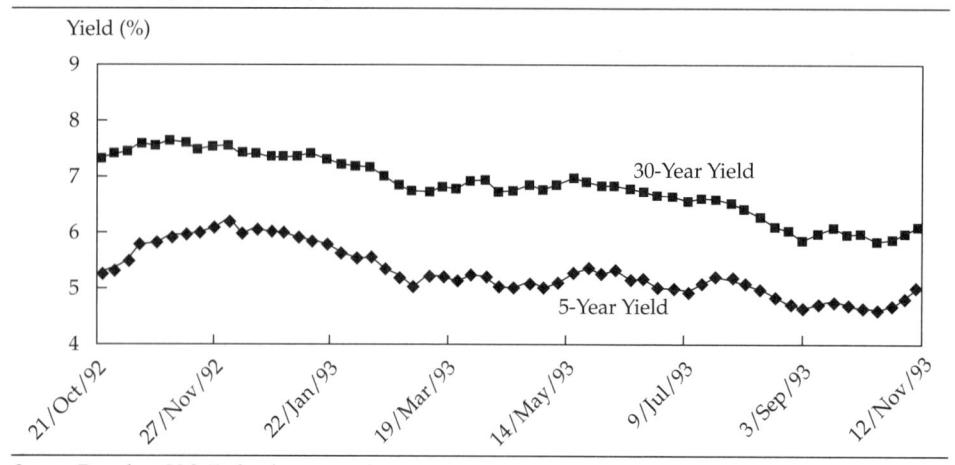

Source: Based on U.S. Federal Reserve data.

Figure 2. Five-Year and Thirty-Year Treasury Yields, November 1993 to May 1994

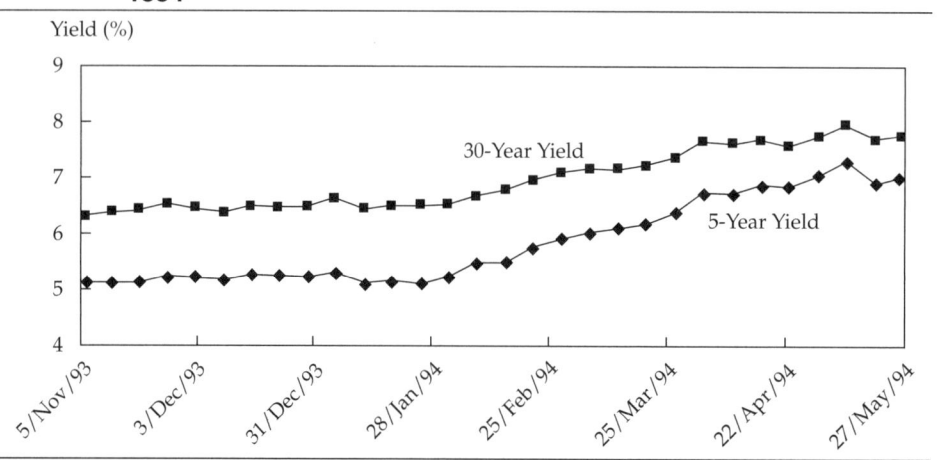

Source: Based on U.S. Federal Reserve data.

An interesting aside to the outcome of the P&G swap story is told in the documents filed in the ensuing lawsuit. The first three months of the swap went well because rates remained stable in November and December 1993 and January 1994. P&G and BT then agreed to amend the terms of the swap. BT offered to change the rate P&G would pay on the swap to CP minus 88 bps plus spread if P&G agreed (which it did) to push back the spread determination date by two weeks, from 4 May to 19 May. The longer the time to expiration for an option, the greater the value of the option, so by accepting the extension to the determination date, P&G was able to write even more valuable options. The two-week extension was made even more valuable because 19 May, the new determination date, was to be preceded by a scheduled Federal Open Market Committee (FOMC) meeting on 17 May and 18 May. (These events were happening during the time period when the target federal funds rate was typically changed only at FOMC meetings.) This marked increase in uncertainty, which raised the value of the option, allowed the swap terms to be adjusted from minus 75 bps to minus 88 bps. And because the interest rate option would now expire after the FOMC meeting, the option became even more valuable.

P&G was engaging in aggressive corporate finance by having a portion of its capital structure intentionally subject to interest rate risk.[2] P&G was

---
[2] For more information on P&G's swap, see Donald J. Smith, "Aggressive Corporate Finance: A Close Look at the Procter & Gamble–Bankers Trust Leveraged Swap," *Journal of Derivatives* (Summer 1997):67–79.

hoping, like many others in the market, to cash in on the stable, upwardly sloping yield curve. Unfortunately, in early February 1994, the Fed started tightening with the first of a series of increases in the federal funds rate as a preemptive strike against future inflation. The rise in rates increased the volatility associated with future interest rates. Because P&G had effectively written options, in order to reverse the swap P&G would need to buy back the options, but only after the May 1994 FOMC meeting. This factor introduced more volatility into an already volatile situation. As a result, the value of the put options written by P&G increased and from P&G's perspective began to move into negative territory.

By February 1994, the value of the swap was negative by about $15 million to $20 million. Rather than closing out the swap and taking the loss, P&G tried to trade its way out by entering into another leveraged swap, this one based on German interest rates. By moving to the German market, P&G completely stepped away from its core competency. P&G took another interest rate bet in the hope that it could extricate the company from both swaps. It was not to be.

The second swap also went south. On a series of different dates in March 1994, P&G closed out both swaps. The pretax charge to earnings to write off the loss on both swaps was $157 million. The size of the loss on the first swap (about $100 million on a notional principal of $200 million) bespoke the leverage that was built into the formula for spread. The swap was closed out as though spread were 1,500 bps and as though P&G were committed to pay the commercial paper rate plus 14.12 percent. In the end, the swap failed miserably simply because of rising rates and volatility (brought on by Fed tightening) combined with the large amount of leverage in the spread formula. And yet, if a relatively simple risk analysis had been done by P&G, the risk to the swap of yields rising 100–150 bps from November 1993 to May 1994 would have been readily apparent.

Swap's Impact on Accounting for Derivatives. The P&G story is important to a discussion of SFAS No. 133 because prior to the new accounting standard, written options could be embedded in swap transactions and accounted for and reported as swap transactions. Thus, swap accounting kept the market value of the underlying derivatives off the balance sheet, thereby removing the powerful influence of transparency on moderating corporate risk taking. If (instead of doing the swap with BT) P&G had structured the same deal using options on Treasury futures contracts traded on the Chicago Board of Trade in a sufficient quantity to generate $6.5 million in premiums (equivalent to the potential funding cost benefit on the original swap) and if P&G had closed out the option positions in March 1994 (i.e., buying the put options back at their market prices on the same dates it had closed out the swap), the most P&G would have lost would have been $30 million to $35 million. Contrast this amount with the $100 million that P&G lost on the original swap. My point is that for the risk that P&G took in the swap with BT, it received only one-third of the premium that it could have received. P&G had clearly entered into a poorly priced speculative deal.

I do not know why P&G would have made such a deal, but the ability to use swap accounting to report the transaction must have been an important motivation. In my opinion, P&G never would have done the deal explicitly because of the accounting that the explicit transaction would have required. In the 1993–94 period, under U.S. GAAP, a written option would not have qualified for hedge accounting. So, if P&G had used options to structure the same deal, the option positions would have been on the balance sheet as a line item, not buried in a swap transaction, and as the market value of those written options became negative to P&G, they would have been marked to market through reported income. My guess is that P&G did not want to show such a transaction. The company did not want the explicit accounting, so it embedded the transaction in a swap.

The logical deduction seems to be that P&G believed that the leveraged swap qualified for "synthetic alteration" treatment. As such, the swap would have been combined with the underlying debt obligation for accounting and reporting purposes and the resulting higher or lower cost of borrowed funds would have been buried in interest expense. The 5.3 percent coupon payment on the debt plus the positive or negative net cash flow on the swap would have become the reported interest expense. The swap would have been reported off balance sheet, in the footnotes, and would have been combined with all other derivatives. An analyst would not have been able to see P&G's big bet on interest rates; the bet would have been buried in the cost of funds. If spread had been zero and the swap had worked, P&G would have known the bet was a home run. But if spread had been 150 bps, so that P&G's interest cost was CP plus 75 bps (i.e., CP minus 75 bps plus spread of 150 bps), which is more than an AA credit such as P&G should have to pay, no analyst or investor ever would have known. The true cost would have been hidden in total interest expense. And the risks associated with obtaining that level of interest expense would have been hidden as well.

Other companies, such as Air Products and Chemicals and Gibson Greetings, were making deals of this ilk—writing options embedded in a swap to get swap accounting treatment. But if the transactions had been done on a stand-alone basis, they would have been accounted for differently. These abuses prompted the U.S. SEC to instruct the FASB to make the necessary changes to get derivatives reported on the balance sheet. The primary motivation behind the resulting accounting standard, SFAS No. 133, was to run any losses on derivatives transactions through income so as to enable the reader of financial statements to see how losses affect earnings. Ironically, this type of mark-to-market accounting and reporting change was a motivating factor in the Enron Corporation debacle. Enron's game was to run the (apparent) gains on derivatives through the income statement to inflate reported earnings.

SFAS No. 133

The major changes made by SFAS No. 133 are that derivatives now must be carried on the balance sheet at fair value; that changes in fair value (realized or not) must flow through the income statement or be carried in other comprehensive income (OCI), which is a component of shareholder equity on the balance sheet; and that the focus is on the type of risk being managed rather than the type of derivative or the source of risk.

The problem that arises in carrying all derivatives, or any instrument that SFAS No. 133 defines as a derivative, on the balance sheet at fair value is determining fair value. No problem exists when good trade prices are available, but when they are not, a valuation model must be used. And when a company uses its own model to value its own derivatives positions, that can open the door to a lack of objectivity. The significant difference between pre- and post-SFAS No. 133 is that prior to SFAS No. 133's adoption, the accounting for derivatives was a piecemeal process; post-SFAS No. 133, this situation is no longer true. Before SFAS No. 133, the accounting for a derivatives transaction was dictated by the particular derivatives product a company used and the particular hedging situation of a company. Now, the central determinant is the type of risk being managed. The accounting and reporting process is no longer product driven but, rather, driven by the source and type of risk.

Types of Risk. The three types of risk that SFAS No. 133 deals with are the exposure to changes in fair value of assets or liabilities already on the balance sheet (or firm commitments), exposure to changes in cash flows on assets or liabilities (or anticipated transactions), and exposure to foreign exchange rates and net investments in foreign operations. I will focus on fair value and cash flow risk but will not discuss foreign exchange rate risk in depth.

Cash flows are stable for fixed-income instruments, so the fair value risk that SFAS No. 133 is concerned with is the potential for change in the value of an asset or liability on a company's balance sheet caused by market conditions. Alternately, for a floating-rate note, the principal value remains stable but the future cash flows change with market conditions. Obviously, these are different types of risk. With fair value risk, the hedge's purpose is to protect against changes in the current value of the asset or liability, and the focus is on the balance sheet. With cash flow risk, the purpose of the hedge is to manage the volatility of future cash flows, and the focus is on the income statement. So, part of a cash flow hedge protects the current year's cash flows, part protects the next year's cash flows, and so on. Thus, the accounting for cash flow risk hedges must accommodate this fundamental difference from accounting for fair value risk hedges, which focus on a single reporting period.

Another way to categorize a transaction is to determine whether the transaction is a firm or an anticipated commitment. If it is a firm commitment with set terms, such as a fixed-rate asset or liability, then the potential changes of concern are changes in the fair value of the contract as a result of changing market conditions. So, changes in the value of a firm commitment can be managed with a fair value hedge.

The other type of transaction is an anticipated transaction. The company views the transaction as highly likely to be undertaken or as part of its normal business procedures. The terms of the transaction, because it is anticipated, are not yet set, so the anticipated transaction is similar to the cash flow hedge because it does not have a fixed value in the present. Thus, changes in the value of anticipated transactions can be managed with a cash flow hedge.

SFAS No. 133 requires that a company specify exactly which risk is being managed in order to choose the proper hedge accounting method. As a result, SFAS No. 133 places enormous demands on companies to think about what they are doing. It effectively says to companies: Before you start dabbling in derivatives, you need to decide if you are hedging or speculating. If you are outright speculating, you will have to show the derivatives at fair value and the gains and losses will flow through the income statement. If you are hedging a financial asset or liability, you have to identify up front which risk is being hedged: market price risk, interest rate risk, foreign exchange risk, or credit risk. If you are hedging a nonfinancial asset, then the risk being hedged is either market price or foreign exchange risk.

"Derivative" Defined. The characteristics of a derivative as outlined by SFAS No. 133 encompass almost every instrument traditionally thought of as a derivative, including futures, options, and swaps. But because companies enter into many nontraditional contracts that have derivative-like provisions, a formal definition was needed. So, how does SFAS No. 133 define a derivative?

A transaction will be classified as a derivative based on the following five characteristics. First, the transaction must have an *underlying*—the element that introduces risk into the transaction and on which changes in the value of the transaction are based. On a typical interest rate swap, the underlying is LIBOR, but it could be the price of oil or the S&P 500 Index. The underlying is the source of a transaction's potential volatility. If the underlying changes, it drives the change in cash flows or fair value.

Second, it must have a notional amount. The notional amount gives the sense of scale of the transaction, for example, an interest rate swap for $100 million. Third, in a derivatives transaction, as the value of the underlying changes, its value changes. Fourth, it must have a small or zero initial net investment. And finally, for a transaction to be classified as a derivative, it must have the ability to be settled on a net basis. If a transaction can be settled only by physical delivery and payment, then it is not a derivative. For example, if the transaction is a forward purchase contract and the only way to settle is by delivery and payment, the transaction does not qualify as a derivative, but if the contract can be settled on a net basis by an observation of the value of the underlying, then the transaction is a derivative.

Examples of Derivatives. Not surprisingly, all instruments traditionally considered derivatives are included in the SFAS No. 133 definition of a derivative—exchange-traded options, futures contracts, OTC forwards, swaps, options on swaps, caps, collars, and floors. The surprise is in the instruments that are not considered to be derivatives. Excluded are traditional insurance products, such as life and property and casualty insurance contracts, even though the contract is clearly an option. Other instruments specifically excluded from classification as a derivative are employee stock options, weather derivatives, and some mortgage-backed securities, such as IO (interest-only) and PO (principal-only) strips. My understanding is that mortgage-backed securities were excluded from SFAS No. 133 because the FASB has chosen to handle them separately because of their significant complexity related to prepayment risk.

Embedded Derivatives. SFAS No. 133 also defines an embedded derivative and mandates specific accounting and reporting treatment for these transactions. The P&G swap contained an embedded derivative: Options were embedded in the swap that was attached to the bond issue. Layers of complexity can disguise when a security contains a derivative that is not "clearly and closely" related to the host instrument. SFAS No. 133 states that when such a situation occurs, the embedded derivative has to be separated (bifurcated) from the rest of the transaction and treated as a stand-alone derivative. A good example is a convertible bond. The equity option that is part of a convertible bond is not clearly and closely related to the host instrument, the bond. Because two different risk exposures are combined in a convertible bond, SFAS No. 133 requires that the bond be valued as a separate instrument and the equity option as a separate instrument. This mandate applies unless the host bond is itself carried at fair value. So, on the one hand, if a bank buys convertibles as part of its trading portfolio and marks the convertible bonds to market, running the change in market value through the income statement, the bank does not have to bifurcate. The fair value risk that SFAS No. 133 set out to capture through accounting requirements is being captured in the mark-to-market valuation. If, on the other hand, the convertible bonds are held as "available for sale" or "hold to maturity," then the reporting of the bonds may have to be bifurcated. Only the investor is required to bifurcate; the issuer of the convertible, however, is not affected by this stipulation.

A typical callable bond does not have to be bifurcated because the call option is not considered to be an embedded derivative. Rather, the value of the call option is deemed to be clearly and closely related to the bond, the host instrument. The same risks—interest rate risk and credit risk—drive both the call option's value and the bond's value, thus meeting the "clearly and closely related" requirement.

Fair Value Hedge

The fair value hedge is designated for assets, liabilities, or firm commitments that have fixed terms—a preset fixed rate or price. A classic example of a fair value hedge begins with a fixed-rate bond. Suppose a company issues a fixed-rate bond but wants to modify the effective interest rate of the bond. The company can do so by entering into a receive-fixed/pay-LIBOR interest rate swap. Such a transaction means that the company is obligated to make fixed-rate interest payments on the note but will receive the same fixed-rate payments on the first leg of the swap, so the two payment streams will cancel each other. The company is then left with the second leg of the swap, the floating-rate leg, as the true financing cost of the underlying fixed-rate note. This transaction transforms the fixed-rate debt to floating-rate debt.

The company may choose this financing technique for several reasons. A prime motivation would be if the company wants to fund a large proportion of its financing needs at the short end of the yield curve (i.e., through the floating-rate note), where interest rates are normally lower than those at the longer end of the yield curve. Studies show that a significant reduction in a company's cost of funds over time can be obtained from shifting a larger part of its debt burden to the short end of the curve.

So, why does a company not issue short-term notes or more commercial paper instead of entering into an elaborate receive-fixed/pay-LIBOR interest rate swap? The problem for companies that issue in the short-term market is the danger of being unable to continuously roll over the debt. Bad news about an issuing company or a general reduction in demand for short-term debt can prohibit a company's access to the commercial paper market just when the company needs this facility the most. The swap enables a company to achieve the same short-term funding cost without exposing itself to the risk of being closed out of the short-term market. Through this type of interest rate swap, a company is able to lock in a longer-term cost of funds with the five-year fixed-rate note, transform the note into a floating-rate note, and thus take advantage of lower short-term rates. It is as though the company were refinancing the medium-term fixed-rate note by continuously rolling over short-term debt. Many companies analyze this strategy from the perspective of their expected cost of funds. From time to time, the interest rate swap is an outright arbitrage in that the company's expected cost to issue floating-rate debt is higher than the cost of acquiring a floating-rate obligation synthetically through an interest rate swap.

The gain or loss on a derivative that is "designated and qualifying" as a fair value hedge is recognized in current earnings together with the offsetting gain or loss on the hedged item for the specific risk being hedged (e.g., interest rate risk but not credit risk). SFAS No. 133 does not allow a company to wait until the end of the year to designate which derivatives will serve as hedges for which risks. The derivative has to be designated at the outset as a hedge and must qualify as a hedge. In order to qualify as a hedge, the transaction has to pass an effectiveness test to determine whether it can be anticipated to be an effective hedge for the risk that is being hedged.

(Note that I will discuss later in detail the test for determining effectiveness.) If the derivative qualifies for effectiveness, then any changes in the underlying host instrument—the bond—and changes in the swap value both will flow to the income statement and the balance sheet and thus offset one another on a net basis. A company can no longer carry its debt modified by the swap at book value; it has to show the carrying value of the debt that will be affected by changes in the risk being hedged. For a fixed-rate bond, only changes in benchmark interest rates can cause a change in carrying value for purposes of hedge accounting. A company's cost of funds can change for many reasons, but only benchmark interest rate changes matter, not changes in credit, because the risk that is being hedged is interest rate risk.

The net result is that earnings are affected only to the extent that the hedge is ineffective. If the hedge is well designed and works as expected, the two offsetting changes (on the underlying and the swap) pass through the income statement, one plus and one minus, and are reflected on the balance sheet, one plus and one minus. To the extent that the hedge is effective, there is no net impact on the financial statements.

Panel A of **Figure 3** illustrates a receive-fixed interest rate swap in which a company has issued a traditional fixed-rate note. The company is receiving a fixed rate (equal to the fixed rate payable on the note) and paying LIBOR. After entering into the swap, suppose that interest rates fall. As a result, the swap now has positive value because the company is receiving a relatively high fixed rate and paying a lower level of LIBOR. The swap becomes a net asset. Panel B of Figure 3 illustrates the positive swap value as an asset on the balance sheet. Likewise, the carrying value of the bond will rise in the lower interest rate environment—the increased value of the note shown on the liability side of the balance sheet. The value of the liability is higher because if the company wanted to buy the note back, it would cost more than the price at which it was issued. Likewise, investors are valuing the note more highly on their own books because the note's price has appreciated with the fall in interest rates. If the hedge works, each side of the balance sheet is affected equally.

Panel C of Figure 3 illustrates the impact of rising rates on the swap. If rates rise, the value of the receive-fixed swap turns negative because the company is receiving a below-market fixed rate. The negative value of the swap, however, is offset by the reduced value of the note. Both changes pass through the income statement and are reflected on the balance sheet. SFAS No. 133 does not state where on the income statement these changes in value should be

Figure 3. Balance Sheet for Fair Value Hedge Example: Receive-Fixed/Pay-LIBOR Swap

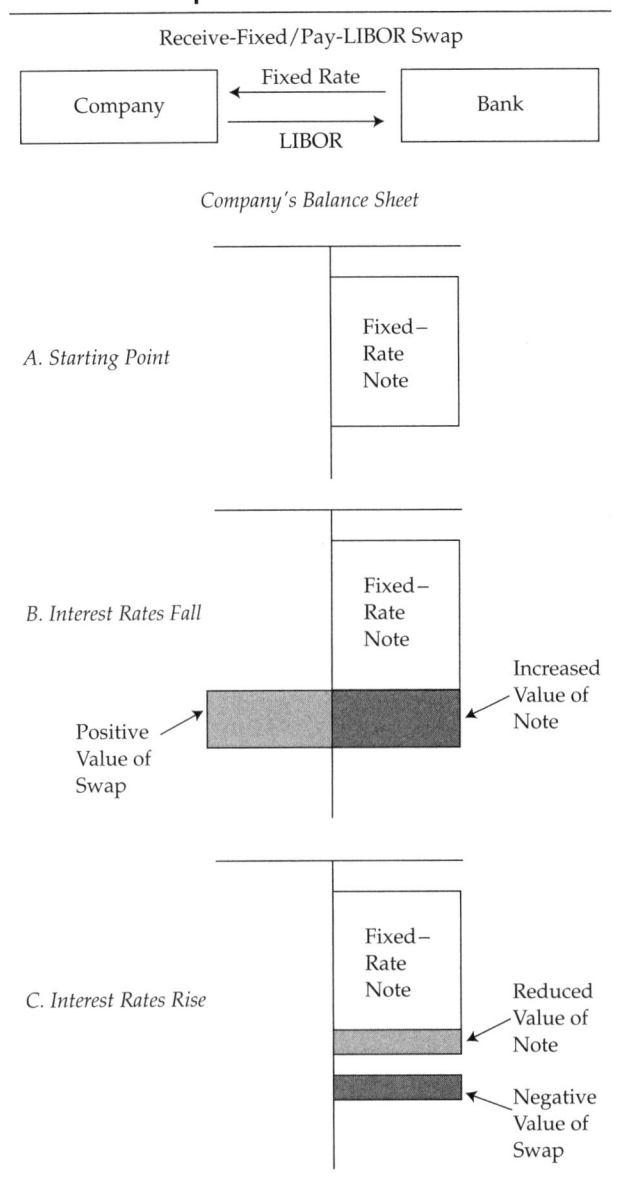

Receive-Fixed/Pay-LIBOR Swap

Company ←Fixed Rate— Bank
        —LIBOR→

Company's Balance Sheet

A. Starting Point
- Fixed-Rate Note

B. Interest Rates Fall
- Fixed-Rate Note
- Increased Value of Note
- Positive Value of Swap

C. Interest Rates Rise
- Fixed-Rate Note
- Reduced Value of Note
- Negative Value of Swap

shown. A company could throw the changes into cost of funds or cost of materials. An analyst needs to know where a company is reporting the change in the value of its derivatives because that could be an element causing the company's financial ratios to change.

Cash Flow Hedge

The cash flow hedge is designated for assets, liabilities, or anticipated (highly probable) transactions that have variable terms, which cause future cash flows associated with the transaction to be uncertain. A classic example of a cash flow hedge begins with a floating-rate note. Suppose a company issues floating-rate debt but does not want the cash flow risk associated with the future stream of variable interest payments. The company can hedge the cash flow risk by entering into a pay-fixed/receive-LIBOR swap. If the company receives LIBOR on the first leg of the interest rate swap, then the LIBOR payment obligation of the company (and the cash flow risk associated with the variable interest expense) is canceled. The second leg of the swap allows the company to pay a fixed rate on its debt. The result is that the floating-rate debt has been synthetically transformed to fixed-rate debt. This interest rate swap can be a classic arbitrage. Many companies claim that they get a lower synthetic fixed rate via the swap market than they would if they simply issued the fixed-rate note directly.

SFAS No. 133 states that the gain or loss on a derivative "designated and qualifying" as a cash flow hedge must be carried in OCI and recycled into earnings in the period when the hedged transaction occurs (e.g., when the future interest payments on the floating-rate bond are paid). Any ineffectiveness in the hedge is run through the income statement and is thus reported in current earnings.

The swap is hedging cash flow risk for each year the floating-rate note is outstanding, so any change in the value of the swap pertains to all future years. The total change is recorded in OCI (in shareholder equity) on the balance sheet, thus allowing the change to be pulled out of equity year by year (or for each interest payment period) on a partial basis as the hedged variable interest payments are made. The cash flow hedge accounting treatment under SFAS No. 133 does not bring the entire change in swap value through income in a single year because the change in swap value represents more than one year's adjustment to interest expense.

Panel A of **Figure 4** illustrates a pay-fixed/receive-LIBOR interest rate swap when a company seeks to hedge the cash flow risk associated with a floating-rate note on its balance sheet. Panel B of Figure 4 shows how the cash flow hedge is reported if interest rates rise. In a higher interest rate environment, the company pays what is now a below-market fixed rate, so the swap takes on a positive value, which is reported as an asset on the balance sheet. And as the value of the swap rises, OCI rises along with it.

If rates fall, the swap decreases in value because the financing cost provided by the swap is higher than market rates. Panel C of Figure 4 shows the negative change in swap value on the balance sheet and the commensurate drop in OCI. Think of OCI as the place where the unrealized gain or loss on the swap is carried. Period by period, a line item on the income statement will adjust the variable cost of

Figure 4. Balance Sheet for Cash Flow Hedge Example: Pay-Fixed/Receive-LIBOR Swap

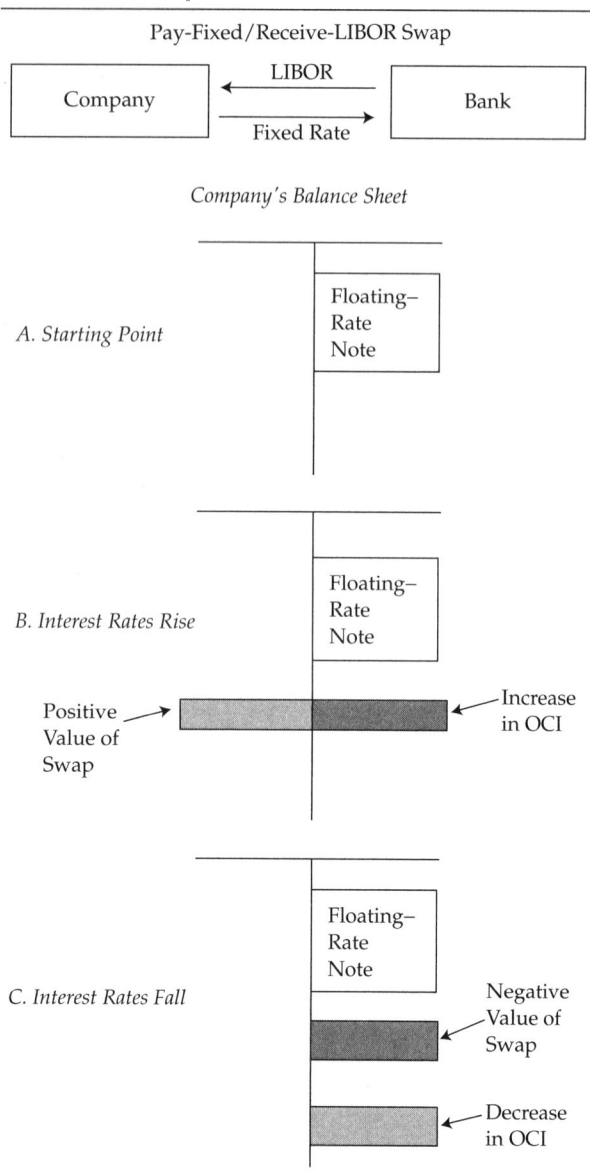

funds to a fixed cost of funds. The adjusting entry will be balanced by an entry adjusting OCI. If at the end of the five-year floating-rate note term the hedge works as planned, the company will have the same interest expense as if it had issued a five-year fixed-rate note.

Effectiveness Testing

The hedge, either a fair value or cash flow hedge, must be expected to be effective at the outset of the transaction, and then its effectiveness must be regularly tested throughout its lifetime. "Effectiveness" typically is interpreted to mean that the change in value of the derivative and the change in value of the underlying remain roughly within an 80–120 percent range of each other, in terms of monetary value; an effective offset is maintained within these bounds. If the hedge is deemed to be ineffective, however, the net positive or negative change in value is reported on the income statement so that the change in value flows through earnings without the counterbalancing offset of a hedged item. The hedge transaction must be marked to market and will affect the reported earnings of the company.

Hedge accounting is complicated, but SFAS No. 133 offers a shortcut method to effectiveness testing. The shortcut method is available only on an interest rate swap intended for use as either a fair value or a cash flow hedge of recognized assets and liabilities. If the derivative and the underlying share the same terms—maturity, payment frequency, settlement date, reference rate, and so on—then the swap is deemed to be perfectly (100 percent) effective. By design, a swap can be structured to mirror the underlying bond. In this case, no effectiveness test is required. The hedge is assumed to be effective, and hedge accounting automatically kicks in with the change in the market value of the derivative matching the carrying value of the hedged instrument. My understanding is that if a deal does not meet the criteria for the shortcut method of effectiveness testing, many corporations will not even consider it. The shortcut treatment eliminates many potential problems.

Conclusion

I would like to conclude by making two observations related to hedging. First, the word "hedge" in accounting is used to imply action taken to *reduce* risk. If a company is hedging, the intent is to reduce risk for the business. SFAS No. 133 has altered this meaning in the sense that reducing risk is not part of the effectiveness test for hedge accounting. Now, the word "hedge" means an action taken to *manage* risk. The hedge itself could be *increasing* risk at the enterprise level. The test put forth under SFAS No. 133 does not ask whether the derivatives are reducing overall enterprise risk but, rather, what type of risk is being hedged—cash flow or fair value risk? In the current environment, "hedge" means an action taken to manage risk; that is all.

Second, the value of a financial asset or liability shown on the balance sheet is neither the original cost nor the current market value. The carrying value simply reflects past hedging actions. Thus, an analyst looking at the reported value of a company's securities cannot know what the company paid for them or what they are currently worth.

Question and Answer Session

Donald J. Smith

Question: Why is the synthetic versus actual difference in the cost of funds not arbitraged away?

Smith: Most academics would answer that question, "of course it is, or will be." And most investors and corporate treasurers would claim that in the short run there are arbitrage opportunities, even though they will disappear at some point.

My alternative explanation is that what companies often view as an arbitrage gain is actually an underreporting of risk. In the synthetic swap structure, there is credit, accounting, and tax risk, none of which is recorded as either part of the swap rate itself or the all-in cost of funds. So, if those risks are not recorded, the company can treat every possible gain as pure arbitrage profit. At least, this is what I think often happens in simple transactions. A more complex structure, however, contains more embedded options and therefore creates a greater possibility of an arbitrage opportunity. For simple, plain-vanilla transactions, however, it is difficult to argue that many opportunities for arbitrage exist.

Question: What items other than the adjustment in value of a cash flow hedge are carried in OCI?

Smith: OCI is a component of shareholder equity and is where companies record changes in the market value of available-for-sale securities if the company is not running these changes through the income statement. OCI is also where a company would record changes in the translated value of foreign assets. To my understanding (I'm not an accountant), it is an account in which a lot of unrealized changes in value are recorded.

Question: Are there any reasons, other than the ones you have already mentioned, a company would choose to enter into an interest rate swap?

Smith: One reason I did not mention would be to attain the optimal debt structure. An interest rate swap can more easily shift a company from fixed-rate to floating-rate debt than can issuing new debt to buy back outstanding debt. In sum, swaps can efficiently restructure the right-hand side of a corporate balance sheet.

The problem in practice is that not much theory exists to guide a corporate treasurer in this regard. Nevertheless, an analysis of the optimal debt structure would begin with a company's operating revenues. A company whose operating revenues float up and down with the level of interest rates should fund with relatively more floating-rate debt. So, when its cost of funds rises, its revenues also rise, and vice versa; the two rise and fall together. Alternatively, if a company's revenues have no apparent correlation with the changing level of interest rates, then the company might be better served by funding with longer-term, fixed-rate debt.

Derivatives and the Enron Debacle

Walter V. Haslett, CFA
President and Chief Investment Officer
Write Capital Management
Philadelphia

> As the derivatives markets grow ever more vast, they play an increasingly critical economic role for purposes of hedging, speculation, and price discovery. Before getting involved, however, investors must thoroughly understand these markets. In particular, they should heed the lessons that can be learned from the well-publicized mistakes of several high-profile companies in which ignorance, poor risk control, inadequate supervision, mismatches between hedged and hedging instruments, and failure to understand the difference between hedging and speculating led to disaster.

The derivatives market is vast and growing larger every year. Derivatives are a permanent feature of the financial landscape, and investors need to learn from past derivatives-related debacles in order to avoid similar problems in the future. This presentation briefly explores these markets and their past catastrophes and examines the role derivatives played in the implosion of the Enron Corporation.

The Derivatives Market

Derivatives are traded in two different marketplaces. The first is an organized exchange for listed derivatives—where buyers meet sellers and trade a standardized product in a regulated market. The second is the OTC market—an unregulated market in which buyers meet sellers and trade a customizable product.

The total outstanding notional value of derivatives at midyear 2002 was $40 trillion on the organized exchanges and $110 trillion on the OTC market (according to data from the Bank for International Settlements). The actual trading volumes, however, are extremely close in both marketplaces, ranging from about $140 to $150 trillion a quarter. To put these numbers in perspective, the annual dollar amount of stocks trading on the NYSE in 2001 was $10.5 trillion. Clearly, the derivatives markets are huge and are growing dramatically every year.

Purposes of Derivatives

Derivatives have three purposes: hedging, speculation, and price discovery. Hedging reduces exposure to the risk of an adverse price movement. In contrast, speculation increases exposure to a risk in order to profit from favorable price movements.

Price discovery's purpose is less obvious but no less significant. A contract in, say, a two-year oil future is a good indication of how the marketplace is valuing the price of oil two years in the future and gives producers and users an opportunity to hedge their risk (i.e., their exposure to a change in the future price of oil). Companies producing resources (such as oil or gold) can sell their anticipated production in the futures market to lock in a certain selling price before the resource is actually sold. Purchasers of the resource can buy to lock in a purchase price for a future need. In this regard, the derivatives market serves an extremely important function.

Problems in the Derivatives Market

Although the derivatives market provides solutions to many problems faced by its users, it also presents several challenges, which generally fall into four categories. First, many of these problems can be attributed to a lack of understanding on the part of the person entering into a derivatives transaction. Some derivatives contracts are straightforward, but others

---

Editor's Note: For further discussion concerning some of the topics addressed in this presentation, see Christopher L. Culp, Merton H. Miller, and Andres M.P. Neves, "Value at Risk: Uses and Abuses," *Journal of Applied Corporate Finance* (Winter 1998):26–38. This article is available at aimrpubs.org in the "2003 CFA Curriculum: Refresher Readings for Charterholders" section: www.aimr.org/memservices/private/pdf/pubs/ValueatRisk.pdf.

are extremely complicated. Managers often become involved in situations such as the Procter & Gamble (P&G) swap, described by Don Smith,[1] in which the managers did not understand the magnitude of the trade to which they were committed.

The second type of problem is poor risk control and supervision once a derivatives transaction has been entered into. The third kind of problem is the mismatch between the hedged and hedging instruments. If an investor wants to hedge a long-term exposure to a particular type of risk, the investor should select an instrument with a maturity as close as possible to the maturity of the exposure that is being hedged. Hedging a long-term exposure with a short-term contract opens the door to substantial problems. Finally, investors frequently do not understand the difference between hedging and speculating. The P&G swap was simply one big speculative trade, but P&G did not grasp the magnitude of the speculation.

Real-Life Examples

The common problems discussed in the previous section are exemplified in five famous (or infamous) derivatives disasters: Orange County,[2] Barings Bank,[3] Metallgesellschaft (MG),[4] Long-Term Capital Management (LTCM),[5] and Enron (note that Enron is addressed in the next section).

Orange County. The Orange County, California, Investment Pool debacle unfolded in December 1994. The loss incurred of $1.6 billion (out of $7.5 billion in invested funds) was 10 times greater than the $160 million loss experienced by P&G and was the largest loss ever recorded by a local government investment pool. Orange County's treasurer, Robert Citron, believed in the early 1990s that he could outperform the market by borrowing short term and lending long term ("playing the yield curve"). In fact, he outperformed the typical county treasurer by 2 percent annually for two years running with this strategy. Citron had made a huge bet that interest rates would remain stable or decline, but in February 1994, the U.S. Federal Reserve pushed interest rates higher as it moved to tighten monetary policy and stave off inflationary pressures (the same interest rate move that caused P&G's swap to go south). Citron's derivatives positions (reverse repurchase agreements and inverse floaters) exploded as long-term rates rose more than short-term rates. The county—one of the most prosperous in the United States—fell into bankruptcy as a result of the devastatingly huge loss. (It has since recovered.)

Citron's problems in the Orange County Investment Pool resulted from a poor understanding of the derivatives he was using—the true vulnerability of the positions in a rising interest rate environment—and inadequate risk control to protect the portfolio's value should an occasion of rising interest rates materialize.

Barings Bank. The story of the end of the 223-year-old Barings Bank is one of the most interesting derivatives catastrophes to date and demonstrates the danger of poor internal controls and supervision. Nick Leeson, a trader and general manager at Barings Futures Singapore, a subsidiary of Barings Bank, was sent to Singapore in 1992 to conduct futures arbitrage on the Japanese stock market index, the Nikkei. He was to purchase a contract that traded on the Singapore International Monetary Exchange (SIMEX) and sell a similar contract that traded in Japan, or vice versa, and thus lock in a trading profit from the arbitrage between the two markets. This approach worked for a while, until Leeson decided that more money could be made by buying contracts in both markets instead of buying one and selling the other. The result was a loss of more than a billion dollars, which was an amount greater than Barings' entire capital and reserves. This loss forced the subsequent sale of Barings to the Dutch bank ING Group for one pound sterling.

Leeson was able to hide his growing losses for nearly two years because of poor internal controls that allowed him to act as both front-office trader and back-office settlements manager.

Metallgesellschaft. The case of MG is not as widely known as the first two examples. MG, a German conglomerate, is a traditional metals company. In 1992, MG began to offer its clients long-term oil contracts of up to 10 years, in which it would guarantee a price above the current spot price. The company initially did well with the contracts, occasionally even booking a profit of $5 a barrel. These contracts, however, created exposure for MG to fluctuations in oil prices over a protracted time period. The company tried to hedge this exposure by buying short-term oil contracts to balance what was essentially a short position in oil maintained on a long-term basis. On

---

[1] Please see Mr. Smith's presentation in this proceedings.
[2] See Philippe Jorion, "Orange County Case: Using Value at Risk to Control Financial Risk" (21 February 2001): www.gsm.uci.edu/~jorion/oc/case.html.
[3] See "Report of the Board of Banking Supervision Inquiry into the Circumstances of the Collapse of Barings" (18 July 1995): www.numa.com/ref/barings/bar00.htm.
[4] See John Digenan, Dan Felson, Robert Kelly, and Ann Wiemert, "Metallgesellschaft AG: A Case Study" *The FMT Review*: www.stuart.iit.edu/fmtreview/fmtrev3.htm.
[5] See David Shirreff, "Lessons from the Collapse of Hedge Fund, Long-Term Capital Management": risk.ifci.ch/146490.htm.

paper, the transaction did look like a hedge, but when oil prices on the short-term contracts came crashing down and prices on the long-term contracts did not, the result was a loss of $1.5 billion.

Unlike Barings, MG was able to weather the derivatives-induced storm that hit it broadside, a storm that arose from a mismatch in the hedged and hedging instruments.

Long-Term Capital Management. The granddaddy of all derivatives fiascos is the hedge fund LTCM, with losses in excess of $2.5 billion. LTCM set up quasi-arbitrage positions, including shorting long-term U.S. government bonds and futures and buying Russian debt to benefit from the widening spread between the two markets. Unfortunately, the spread moved even wider when Russia defaulted in August 1998 and the trades became extremely unprofitable. They also experienced losses in other areas, such as mortgage-backed securities and equity index options. The hedge fund's loss was so large that the U.S. Federal Reserve had to negotiate a privately funded bail-out in which some of the largest financial institutions in the United States and Europe invested more than $3.5 billion in capital.

This case is particularly fascinating because of the pedigree of LTCM. The firm's founder, John Meriwether (formerly of Salomon Brothers), was considered one of the best bond traders in the world. Among his partners were two Nobel Prize winners, Myron Scholes and Robert Merton, and a former vice chairman of the U.S. Federal Reserve Bank, David Mullins. They believed in their models and continued to believe in them far longer than they should have. During the unusual market conditions that occurred in August of 1998, the previously observed relationship between financial instruments broke down, resulting in a financial disaster that will long be remembered.

The Case of Enron

In the 1990s, Enron earned accolades for being one of the most successful companies in the world. *Fortune* named Enron the most innovative company in the world for five years (from 1996 to 2000). In 2000, Enron was named 24th on *Fortune*'s list of the 100 best companies to work for in America. During this period, Enron was also ranked by *Fortune* as number one in management quality and number two in employee talent. Andrew Fastow was even named one of the CFOs of the year by *CFO Magazine* in 1999.[6]

---

[6]See Russ Banham, "How Enron Financed Its Amazing Transformation from Pipelines to Piping Hot," *CFO Magazine* (1 October 1999): www.cfomagazine.com/article/1,5309,1340||M|305,00.html.

This company profited from a wealth of talent, or so it seemed, among its management.

A root cause of Enron's trouble was its rapid growth in the 1990s. Unfortunately, this rapid growth required large capital outlays, and Enron was faced with a dilemma. Management did not want to issue additional debt because of the amount already outstanding. Nor did management want to issue more stock, for doing so would dilute earnings. Because Enron was so active in the derivatives market, particularly in the OTC derivatives market, the company had to ensure that it remained highly creditworthy in the eyes of its trading partners. Whereas the listed market has an organization that guarantees trades, the OTC market does not; trades are entered into solely based on the creditworthiness of the counterparty (i.e., the other side of the trade). So, if Enron's creditworthiness was perceived to be questionable, no one would be willing to trade with it. Thus, Enron decided to create the now infamous special purpose entities (SPEs) to keep certain financing activities off of its financial statements.

Special Purpose Entities. SPEs are separate legal entities, whether a corporation, partnership, or trust. In order to warrant off-balance-sheet treatment, an entity must have 3 percent outside ownership and control must be exercised by the independent owner. If those two conditions are met, a great deal of reporting manipulation is possible. Debt can be transferred to the SPE from the parent company and thus can be taken off the parent's balance sheet. Gains can be recognized on the income statement of the parent by selling the assets of the parent company to the SPE. Not all SPEs are bad. They first gained popularity in the 1970s and 1980s and are primarily used for synthetic lease transactions; sales of financial assets; structured-finance, asset-backed securities; and hedging activities.

Three large SPEs were the primary cause of problems for Enron, one of which was Chewco Investments, named for the tall, furry character Chewbacca in the *Star Wars* movies. Chewco was set up in November 1997 to facilitate Enron's buyout of CalPERS' stake in a partnership known as JEDI—the Joint Energy Development Investment. Michael Kopper (at that time, Enron's director of global finance) managed Chewco, which did not comply with the nonconsolidation rules because neither the 3 percent outside ownership nor the independent director existed.

The LJM Limited Partnerships (LJM 1 & 2) were created in 1999 and were managed by Andrew Fastow, Enron's CFO. Like Chewco, LJM was not in compliance with the nonconsolidation rules and did not qualify for off-balance-sheet treatment.

The third SPE, created in 2000, was Raptors (I, II, III, and IV). Raptors' purpose was to hedge part of Enron's merchant banking exposure. Like Chewco and LJM, Raptors did not meet the nonconsolidation rules and did not qualify for off-balance-sheet treatment. Nevertheless, Enron chose not to comply with GAAP in reporting the activities of the SPEs and kept all associated transactions off its books. For a while, Enron successfully used the SPEs to conceal debt, book phantom profits, and provide the illusion of hedging its risk in certain equity investments. The use of SPEs misrepresented Enron's financial statements and deceived everyone involved—employees, investors, and analysts—long enough for many of Enron's executives to sell their Enron stock before the price plummeted.

One Slice of Deception. Enron's complicated use of derivatives and SPEs can make even a 20-year derivatives veteran's head spin. As an example, consider one of Enron's straightforward trades.

This slice of deception, called Rhythms Net Communications, was the first business deal between Enron and LJM1. In fact, the Rhythms transaction marked the first time that Enron transferred its own stock to an SPE to use as a hedging vehicle and the first example of how an "arms-length" transaction between Enron and LJM was structured to provide favorable terms to LJM.

In March 1998, Enron invested $10 million in the purchase of 5.4 million shares (an average of $1.85 a share) of Rhythms stock. About a year later, in April 1999, the company went public with an IPO of $21 a share. The share price eventually rose to $69. So, in a little more than a year, Enron earned a gain of more than $300 million on its investment in Rhythms.

The problem was that any fluctuation in Rhythms' stock price would pass through to Enron's income statement and affect reported earnings. Enron would have preferred to sell the stock, but it was unable to do so because of a lockup agreement that required it to hold the stock until November 1999. Enron wanted to hedge its exposure to any dramatic fluctuation in the stock price. Because of the recent issuance and stock listing, no exchange-traded hedging instruments were available. The large size of the position also contributed to making it virtually impossible to commercially hedge in the OTC market. But Rhythms' stock price was highly volatile and the need to hedge was immediate.

In June 1999, Fastow presented a proposal to Enron's board that would allow Enron to hedge the Rhythms stock position by creating the LJM partnership. The partnership was structured as follows: Enron transferred 3.4 million shares of restricted Enron stock (worth approximately $276 million) and cash to LJM1, which, in turn, created a swap subsidiary called LJM Swap Sub. LJM1 was prohibited from selling the Enron stock for four years and could not hedge the stock by other means for one year. In making the transfer to the LJM partnership, Enron discounted the value of its stock by about 40 percent to $168 million and, in exchange, LJM gave Enron a note for $64 million. In addition, Enron received a put option from LJM Swap Sub that allowed Enron to sell the Rhythms stock back to LJM at $56 a share until June 2004. If the stock's price fell, Enron would lose money on the decline in market value but would make money on the hedge, which would mitigate the fluctuations on Enron's income statement. In other words, the put would lock in a substantial portion of the gain Enron had in Rhythms. During the third and fourth quarters of 1999, the hedge worked as planned when Rhythms' price dropped.

This hedge, however, had several problems. First, the hedge was only an accounting hedge, not an economic hedge. Essentially, Enron funded the LJM SPE as a mechanism to provide a hedge for itself. An economic hedge would have occurred if Enron had purchased a put from a third party (not a self-funded SPE), but Enron essentially bought a put from itself. As Rhythms' stock price declined, LJM's liability on the put grew as the put became more and more valuable. But because the only asset owned by LJM was the Enron stock originally transferred to the partnership, as Enron's stock price dropped, LJM was unable to ante up the money it owed Enron on the put.

In November 2001, Enron admitted that LJM Swap Sub was not properly capitalized and was not correctly treated as a nonconsolidated SPE. As a result, Enron was forced to take a charge to earnings of $95 million in 1999 and $8 million in 2000. Because the lockup agreement on the Rhythms stock was set to expire in November 1999, Enron (at the time it had entered into the "hedge" with LJM) needed to keep the transaction together for only six months. Unfortunately, it was not able to sustain the arrangement even for six months.

The charges from the Rhythms transaction were not the only bad news for Enron in 2001. On 16 October 2001, Enron announced "changes" to its financial statements because of transactions with LJM2—a $544 million after-tax ($710 million pretax) charge against earnings in 2000 and 2001 and a $1.2 billion reduction in shareholder equity. The $1.2 billion reduction in shareholder equity was mainly from the Raptors SPE, which involved a hedge for Enron's merchant investments that was similar to the

Rhythms hedge. In order to hedge the merchant investments, Enron again transferred its own stock to Raptors, set up "hedging" strategies with a self-funded entity, and crossed its fingers. The merchant investments often were simply exchange-traded equity securities, but they also consisted of energy-trading profits that Enron had earned and was trying to lock in. A majority of Enron's earnings came from energy-trading profits, which, of course, fluctuated based on market movements. Again, the "hedge" did not work. The result was the $1.2 billion reduction in Enron's shareholder equity that catapulted Enron into the headlines.

The total Chewco and LJM1 restatements were substantial. Enron's net income took a hit of $28 million in 1997, $133 million in 1998, $248 million in 1999, and $99 million in 2000. Shareholder equity decreased by $258 million in 1997, $391 million in 1998, $710 million in 1999, and $754 million in 2000. Debt was restated upward by $711 million in 1997, $561 million in 1998, $685 million in 1999, and $628 million in 2000. These write-downs were necessary because the SPEs were originally treated as nonconsolidated entities. Once the reality of the situation became apparent, Enron was forced to restate prior-year financial results because the previous off-balance-sheet reporting of the SPEs was not appropriate; the 3 percent requirement for outside ownership was not met.

The net income restatements ranged from 10 to 20 percent of Enron's net annual income. The shareholder equity restatements ranged from 5 to 7 percent of total shareholder equity, and the debt restatements ranged from 7 to 11 percent of total outstanding debt. Remember the implications of such serious negative restatements for a company dependent on dealing in the OTC derivatives market. The need to be a strong, creditworthy counterparty is critical, and major restatements of this nature totally destroy any possible perception of creditworthiness.

Lessons

The Powers Report[7] is the investigative report prepared by the special investigative committee of Enron's board of directors. The report states that the board members tried to be diligent but were bamboozled by extremely clever financial professionals—those same professionals widely touted for their talent and financial acumen.[8] Nevertheless, as the saying goes, "once burnt, twice shy," and by heeding the lessons of Enron, investors can better detect the warning signs of derivatives disasters.

As indicated by the current size and rate of growth in the derivatives market, derivatives are an extremely important tool for hedging risk. Investors who use derivatives must make certain that the hedge is a real (economic) hedge, not simply an accounting hedge.

To prevent other derivatives-driven catastrophes, investors should have direct contact with, or even visit, companies; carefully scrutinize the footnotes to the financial statements; and always ask the right questions. Some of these questions are: Do you have any nonconsolidated SPEs on your books? Do you have any officers or employees who have any financial involvement with the SPEs? How close to the 3 percent ownership threshold of qualifying for off-balance-sheet treatment is the SPE? Some regulatory bodies are talking about raising the level for outside ownership of SPEs to 10 percent. In the case of Enron, however, even if the required outside ownership level had been 10 percent, management would have probably devised a way to create the appearance of meeting the threshold.

Investors should be especially careful in analyzing the footnotes to a company's financial statements. Enron was extremely effective at hiding its transactions in its annual reports, 8-Ks, and 10-Qs. Enron's footnotes constituted about one-third of its annual report, so even with the substantial amount of information that was available, many experienced analysts were unable to decipher the wrongdoings until it was too late.

Consider some of the following red flags that appeared in Enron's footnotes:

- "[A] senior officer of Enron is managing member of LJM's general partner." This item was only one line in 20–25 pages of footnotes.
- "The terms of the transactions with related parties are representative of terms that would be negotiated with unrelated third parties." This sentence means that Enron's trades could have been done with a third party; instead, the trades were done internally. The fact that they chose not to use a third party was highly questionable.

And according to the Powers Report, "The notes glossed over issues concerning the potential risks and

---

[7]William C. Powers, Jr., Raymond S. Troubh, and Herbert S. Winokur, Jr., "Report of Investigation by the Special Investigative Committee of the Board of Directors of Enron Corp." (1 February 2002): news.findlaw.com/wp/docs/enron/specinv020102rpt1.pdf.

[8]For a more detailed account of Andrew Fastow's conduct in particular, see *U.S. SEC v. Andrew S. Fastow*, available online at news.findlaw.com/hdocs/docs/enron/secfastow100202cmp.pdf.

returns of the transactions, their business purpose . . . and contingencies involved." Investors should read the Powers Report. It is a highly valuable investigation of one of the most fascinating cases in business history.

Enron is still operating, but whether it will ever emerge from bankruptcy is unknown.

Conclusion

The derivatives markets are huge and continue to grow dramatically. They play a critical economic role for purposes of hedging, speculation, and price discovery. But investors must understand these markets before getting involved in them. Some investors have suffered grievously in the derivatives markets as a result of ignorance, poor risk control, inadequate supervision, mismatches between hedged and hedging instruments, and failure to understand the difference between hedging and speculating.

Note that many of the debacles I described were ultimately precipitated by a trigger event. The P&G and Orange County catastrophes occurred because of a dramatic increase in interest rates. The decline in Japanese equity prices that ultimately caused the ruin of Barings Bank was triggered by the Kobe earthquake. The LTCM trigger event was the Russian moratorium on debt payment, which caused a widening in credit spreads, and in the case of Enron, the real trigger event was the decline in the stock market. This decline caused the price of Enron stock to drop, resulting in an inability to provide the intended hedging benefits to its merchant investments. If these trigger events had never occurred, many of these company's names might never have become synonymous with corporate disasters and scandal. If managements in these cases had had a better understanding of how certain events might have affected their transactions or if they had had better risk controls in place, the catastrophes might have been averted. In the future, investors, analysts, managers, and traders can all benefit from the lessons embedded in these corporate mishaps.

The Current and Future State of Financial Reporting

Patricia A. McConnell
Senior Managing Director
Bear, Stearns & Company, Inc.
New York City

> In the past 30 years, the change from a principle-based system to a rule-based system led to both improvements and complications in financial reporting. The quality and amount of information available to analysts were enhanced, but questions have emerged about issues related to earnings quality. Major unresolved problems include the treatment of special purpose entities, synthetic leases, employee stock options, the form and content of financial statements, revenue recognition, and smoothing of earnings volatility.

The investment community's view of the importance of financial reporting has shifted 180 degrees. Not long ago, clients did not want to hear me discuss my latest theories on financial reporting. Today, they are more receptive. Following the recent debacles of WorldCom and the Enron Corporation, the media have declared a crisis of confidence in the financial community. But I think the crisis is over; the investment community has realized that it is as much to blame for the excesses as are corporate managements, accountants, and auditors. The financial community has realized that to protect itself, its members—the investors and analysts themselves—must be the first line of defense. And part of that defense entails conducting solid financial statement analysis, an idea that can be traced back to Benjamin Graham and David Dodd's 1934 book on security analysis.[1]

The issues that have been cited as the underlying causes for this recent "crisis" are not new. The parallels between the situation now and at the beginning of my career in the early 1970s are amazing, but the solutions being proposed now are quite different. In the 1960s, the United States experienced an economic boom similar to that of the 1990s, and it too led to a number of excesses. As the boom turned into a recession, many of those excesses became apparent and resulted in a number of financial debacles at the end of the 1960s and into the 1970s—just as happened in the late 1990s and into this century. These earlier debacles involved such companies as National Student Marketing, Stirling Homex Corporation, U.S. Financial Corporation, Equity Funding Corporation of America, W.T. Grant Company, and to put the frosting on the cake, Penn Central Corporation.

Evolving Accounting Guidelines

During the late 1960s and early 1970s, just as today, federal regulators sought to find the root cause of the problems and found the accountants to be the primary villains. As a result, in the early 1970s, in order to protect investors in the future, a number of blue-ribbon panels were formed to propose changes to the structure of the U.S. accounting and auditing profession. One panel, the Trueblood Committee, led by Robert Trueblood, formulated a set of basic accounting concepts and issued a report that was the forerunner of the concept statements that currently make up the Financial Accounting Standards Board's (FASB's) conceptual framework. Perhaps the most important of those concepts is that the primary users of financial statements are investors and that the purpose of financial statements is to provide information useful in predicting future cash flows to investors.

At that time, the accounting standard setter was the Accounting Principles Board (APB). The APB

---

[1] Benjamin Graham and David Dodd, *Security Analysis* (New York: McGraw-Hill Companies, 1934).

issued opinions on accounting principles. Some of those APB principles remain in place today; for example, APB No. 25 uses the intrinsic value method to measure the value of employee stock options, allowing companies to avoid recognizing an expense when they grant options to employees.

The APB Opinions were short, only a few pages. Each principle was stated in a few paragraphs, and the remaining pages were devoted to explaining why the principle was needed. The APB Opinions would often include a rebuttal from one of the members of the APB, but the statement was short and to the point. At the end of the 1960s and into the early 1970s, many people felt that a primary cause of the financial debacles was the principle-based accounting rules issued by the APB. The general feeling was that preparers of financial statements and their auditors needed more guidance to apply the principles on a consistent basis to like transactions. Merely stating the principle was insufficient because reasonable people could interpret the facts in such a way that the principle would not apply. Therefore, more implementation guidance was needed.

Another criticism of the APB was the perception that it was not independent enough. The APB, which was a standing committee of the American Institute of Certified Public Accountants (AICPA), the professional organization of CPAs, was considered to be controlled by what were then the "Big Eight" accounting firms, and these firms were considered to be controlled by their clients. Clearly, it was argued, the United States needed an independent accounting standard setter, one that was above the influence of preparers, auditors, and most important, the government.

In response to these concerns, the Wheat Committee, chaired by Francis Wheat, was formed in 1971 to evaluate the APB and propose changes. The Wheat Committee's recommendations led to the dissolution of the APB and the formation of the FASB in 1973. The FASB is a not-for-profit independent organization with seven full-time board members.

The FASB, in response to the criticisms of its predecessor, the APB, decided that the standards it issued needed to provide more implementation guidance. The history of this principle- versus rule-based debate is particularly relevant to the current situation because a similar debate will occur over the next year or so. Although every accounting standard the FASB has ever issued is based on a principle, the difference between the accounting standards set by the APB (or, for that matter, by the International Accounting Standards Board [IASB]) and the FASB is that the FASB standards not only state the principle, as did the APB Opinions, but also provide a great deal of implementation guidance, or rules. The rules exist for two purposes—to make sure people understand the principle and to "scoundrel proof" the principle.

U.S. accounting rules have thus gone from being almost entirely principle based in the early 1970s, when they were issued with little implementation guidance, to being entirely principle based, but with more implementation guidance than anyone had ever imagined. For example, Statement of Financial Accounting Standards (SFAS) No. 133, *Accounting for Derivative Instruments and Hedging Activities*, which was issued in 1998, is based on the principle that all financial derivatives should be carried on the balance sheet at fair value, with changes in fair value recognized in the income statement.[2] If the FASB had stopped there, SFAS No. 133 would have appeared to be simple.

When the FASB proposed this principle, however, the preparer community, the auditor community, and the U.S. Congress demanded more information on how they were supposed to apply the principle. In addition, preparers and auditors complained that most of these derivatives were used in a company's risk management and hedging activities, and if they were marked to market, a mismatch would result because many of the hedged transactions were accounted for at historical cost. So, the FASB included an exception to the principle to allow special hedge accounting when the derivative is designated and qualifies as a hedge. Of course, an exception to a principle requires criteria (another name for rules) for when the exception applies. As a result, SFAS No. 133 includes roughly 1,000 pages of implementation guidance, most of which are devoted to defining a financial derivative (as opposed to a plain financial instrument or a plain derivative) and explaining when and how the special hedge accounting rules may be applied.

A principle-based concept works only if there are no exceptions. With SFAS No. 133, for example, the FASB would not have been able to institute special hedge accounting for derivatives if it wanted to maintain a pure, principle-based system. Furthermore, even if the FASB were to issue principles with few rules, some other regulatory organization would step into the void because the principles must be scoundrel proof. That is, somebody has to make sure that the principles are being consistently applied to transactions that are economically equivalent, even if the transactions have a few different bells and whistles. In the current structure, if the FASB did not supply the rules, the U.S. SEC would most likely do it. As

---

[2] For a summary of SFAS No. 133, see Appendix C.

long as there are scoundrels, society will demand rules to thwart them.

The debate about whether analysts, as users of financial statements, want purely principle-based accounting rules warrants close attention. The results, if the principle-based argument wins the day, may be difficult to accept. With fewer rules, preparers and auditors would have to exercise more, not less, "professional judgment," which could lead to similar transactions being accounted for differently. Controversy would arise over which treatment was more appropriate and which produced the better quality earnings; thus, analysts and investors would have to exercise more professional judgment as well.

Quality of Financial Reporting

The quality of financial reporting is another issue that has cycled around again. The idea of quality financial reporting is often confused with the idea of quality earnings. Having quality financial reporting means not only having clearly stated principles that can be understood and applied in such a way that similar economic transactions are accounted for in a similar manner by all parties but also having financial statements that are transparent enough for the user to understand the economics of the transactions. The concept of earnings quality can best be understood by thinking of it as a spectrum: The highest-quality earnings are the cash earnings (which never have to be returned) received in a transaction that can be repeated with a high level of certainty for every period into the foreseeable future, and the lowest-quality earnings are those that have not yet materialized in the form of cash and that come from a transaction that is not certain to be repeated in the future. In between these extremes is a full spectrum of different earnings qualities.

In my opinion, the quality of financial reporting is higher than it has ever been—high enough that analysts and investors are now able to see the quality of earnings more clearly than in the past. The first company assigned to me when I started in this business was IBM. In the early 1970s, IBM's financial statements were approximately 10 pages long, including the president's letter, balance sheet, and income statement. The financial statements did not contain a cash flow statement; it was not required. They did not contain management's discussion and analysis (MD&A), and they had few footnotes. At that time, IBM was the largest company in the world. Would analysts today be satisfied with a financial statement that was 10 pages, with no cash flow statement or MD&A? Would they even know where to begin to analyze this company? Take the example of pension accounting. Pension accounting has received a great deal of criticism lately, but until the late 1980s, no standard for pension accounting even existed. Analysts had no idea how a company was accounting for its pension plan. Most companies simply expensed whatever they contributed to their pension plan that year, and they contributed whatever amount they wished, within certain boundaries. A company could manage its earnings by the contributions it made to its pension plan, and it would be undetectable.

Not surprisingly, no one can persuade me that financial reporting is of poorer quality today than it was even 10 years ago. In fact, it is better, which has led to the perception that the quality of earnings is lower because investors and analysts now know what items are included in earnings. Five, ten, or fifteen years ago, investors had much less information. The United States did not have standardized rules for pension accounting until 1987. Companies were not required to consolidate all majority-owned subsidiaries until 1989. Cash flow statements were not required until 1989. Retiree health care benefits did not have to be accounted for using accrual accounting until 1993. Codified rules for when to recognize an asset impairment or how to measure the loss did not exist until 1996. Rules on how to account for derivatives did not exist until 2000. And a business combination could be accounted for in two alternative ways until 2001.

Some people say they would like to return to the "good old days," when they could rely on the U.S. GAAP earnings number, put a multiple on it, and know what the company was worth. Such people need to think about what they are wishing for. GAAP earnings were a lot more flexible 10, 15, and even 5 years ago than they are today. Analysts might not like the earnings measure that they get from GAAP, but at least today they have a better idea of what is in that earnings number. Analysts and investors are now able to decompose earnings into high- and low-quality earnings and give high-quality earnings a good multiple and low-quality earnings a low multiple. Today's market multiple is actually a blended or weighted average of the company's high- and low-quality earnings.

The FASB Agenda

Despite the media's attention to the troubles of such companies as Enron and WorldCom, the issues on the FASB's agenda have not changed. The issues that have been pinpointed as the underlying causes of the problems at Enron—incomplete and incomprehensible disclosures, off-balance-sheet financing, revenue recognition, and particularly fair value accounting—are not new. In fact, these issues have been on the FASB's agenda since the 1960s. The FASB has been making small changes over the years, all of which have been intended to improve financial reporting.

Special Purpose Entities. In recent years, special purpose entities (SPEs) have acquired a bad reputation because they often result in off-balance-sheet financing. I do not believe, however, that they are inherently evil. An SPE is any entity, whether a corporation, partnership, or trust, whose purpose is narrowly defined and set out in its corporate charter, partnership agreement, or trust documents. There are sound business and economic reasons for an organization to use an SPE to engage in a particular transaction, and the legal and economic benefits are not negated if the organization has to consolidate the SPE onto its balance sheet. For example, an SPE is often used by a parent company to isolate an activity, asset, or operation from the bankruptcy of its core business. An SPE keeps the transferred assets or operations legally distanced from the original company. This allows the parent to borrow, using the assets as collateral, often at a much lower interest rate. An SPE also allows the risk of holding a particular asset to be diversified by directing its cash flows to investors with different risk tolerances. Consolidation might negate the financial reporting benefits that existed in the past from off-balance-sheet financing, but the substantial economic and legal benefits derived from using an SPE are not lost. The FASB's project on SPEs will require consolidation of only certain SPEs, with synthetic leases among those most likely to be affected.

Synthetic Leases. From a financial accounting standpoint, a synthetic lease is merely a type of operating lease. The primary difference between a synthetic lease and a traditional operating lease is that in a synthetic lease, the lessee reaps the tax benefit—the deductions for depreciation and interest—whereas in an ordinary operating lease, the tax benefit goes to the lessor. Operating leases are a classic form of off-balance-sheet financing, and because a synthetic lease is an operating lease, synthetic leases have never been hidden from analysts. Since the mid-1970s, operating-lease obligations have been disclosed in a footnote that spells out the company's commitments for the next five years by year and then in one lump sum. Anybody paying attention to that footnote has no reason to be concerned about companies potentially consolidating synthetic leases into their financial statements.

Employee Stock Option Compensation. The issue of employee stock option compensation is not officially on the FASB agenda yet, but I believe the FASB plans to deal with it by requiring the fair value method of accounting for options. The first step down this road was taken in September, when the FASB released a statement formally acknowledging its intention to bring its financial accounting standards in line with those of the IASB. On 7 November 2002, the IASB released an exposure draft requiring the fair value method of accounting for options.[3] The FASB's intention of aligning its standards with those of the IASB, along with the fact that the European Commission has issued a directive requiring publicly traded European companies to adopt international accounting standards by 2005, will ease the way for the FASB to adopt the fair value method for stock options in the name of international accounting harmonization.

Other Issues

A number of issues that I have not yet addressed are probably more important in the long run than today's hot topics. Among them are the form and content of financial statements, revenue recognition, and smoothing volatility in earnings.

The Form and Content of Financial Statements. In my opinion, no satisfactory solution exists to the perennial question of who has the most accurate earnings figure—GAAP, First Call Corporation, Standard & Poor's, or the analyst down the block. I believe that what is important is that the company being analyzed provide an income statement in a standard format that contains the line items necessary for an analyst to untangle that income statement for use in analysis and valuation. With this information, an analyst can decide which parts of the earnings are high or low quality and can value the earning streams appropriately. GAAP today provides almost no guidance about the form and content of the income statement and no guidance on what line items should appear or what should be included in those line items. No agreed-upon definition exists, even for something as basic to financial analysis as operating earnings. Fortunately, the FASB and the IASB both have initiated projects for revising the form and content of financial statements. If these boards make the right decisions, investors will get better information on the face of the income

---

[3] The exposure draft "ED 2 Share-Based Payment" was released on 7 November 2002. It could become effective by the end of 2003 as a voluntary standard and be adopted as a rule in Europe in 2005. The proposal may be viewed at www.iasc.org.uk/cmt/.

statement to help assess the quality of the company's earnings. If they make the wrong decision, the investment community will be in deep trouble.

Revenue Recognition. Another issue that deserves attention is revenue recognition. Revenue, as everyone knows, is the single most important number on the income statement. The blame for the recent accounting and reporting problems has focused on the management of earnings through the use of pension accounting, employee stock options, or off-balance-sheet financing, but more than 70 percent of the financial debacles over the past two decades have been driven by revenue-recognition issues.

Revenue-recognition problems occur at different levels, from recording false revenue (e.g., by recording a sale to a customer that does not exist), which is clearly fraudulent, to grayer areas of revenue recognition. Say, for example, a company has a legitimate order from a legitimate, creditworthy customer (perhaps the customer has even paid up front) and the company has the inventory in the warehouse but cannot get the order on the truck by the stroke of midnight at the end of the quarter. So, the company holds its books open until the next morning. Under the current U.S. legal system, the management of that company is equally as culpable as the one that records a sale to a nonexistent customer. To my mind, however, the implications for valuation are different. The first company has no revenue; with the second company, it is simply a question of the length of the accounting period. If the company did not have to report quarterly, it would have made no difference if the goods were shipped on March 31 or April 1. The problem is caused by trying to allocate a continuous process (selling goods to customers) to specified, and somewhat arbitrary, time periods.

The grayest area of revenue recognition arises from the application of GAAP to new and evolving products, services, and/or customer arrangements. This is the grayest area of all.

The FASB has recently, and I believe reluctantly, added a project on revenue recognition to its agenda. The basic problem is that in the United States, there is no accounting standard for revenue recognition. Revenue recognition can be thought of as a generally accepted accounting principle. The principle simply states that revenue should be recognized when earned and when collection is probable. A number of industry-specific rules define when the earnings process is complete for a given industry, but not all industries have these specialized rules. Thus, many companies are left without any guidance. Practices in these industries evolve from an analogy to other industries' guidance or simply as a result of reasoning from the basic principle. The consequence is a patchwork quilt of revenue-recognition practices that appear to lack a coherent thread.

The FASB is addressing this problem conceptually from both the top down and the bottom up. From the bottom up, the FASB is examining all of the industry-specific rules and practices to determine whether a consistent thread runs through them. (I certainly do not see a common thread.) From the top down, it is working with its conceptual framework to develop a consistent approach. So, in the long term, there may be changes to the rules governing revenue recognition that will have a tremendous impact on a company's reported earnings—and thus on its valuation.

In the short term, however, a significant problem area for the financial community is the disagreement among preparers, the SEC, and auditors about how a company should legitimately recognize revenue in certain types of transactions, particularly those that involve multiple deliverables. For example, a company enters into an arrangement with a customer to provide a tangible product, an intangible product, and a related service for a monthly payment of $99.99 for the next 10 years. How should that monthly payment be allocated to the various products and services being delivered? When is the revenue earned? Should the company divide the revenue among each element of the transaction or spread the revenue over the contract life? This issue is tremendously controversial and is being dealt with by the FASB's Emerging Issues Task Force (EITF). The EITF is working to finalize a consensus opinion that could have a material effect on the way many companies recognize revenue in the future.

Smoothing Earnings Volatility. An important question that is not on the FASB's agenda, but should be, is: Who should be responsible for smoothing—accountants or analysts? The concept of smoothing the effect of the peaks and valleys of economic and equity market cycles on a company's transactions has led to controversy about nonrecurring items and about pension accounting. More than a decade ago, the FASB concluded that, in the area of pension accounting, it was appropriate for management to smooth out the volatility inherent in the results of a defined-benefit pension plan. Accordingly, the smoothing mechanisms that dampen the effect of the return on plan assets during rising markets create a cushion in falling markets. Those same smoothing rules, however, are a drag on earnings as the markets level out.

If the FASB had concluded that it was not appropriate for accountants to smooth earnings, then earnings would reflect what the pension assets actually earned every period. I believe market participants would quickly have realized that these were stock market returns (normally considered poor-quality earnings) and would not have placed a normal operating multiple on pension income. Multiples might not have gotten as wildly out of line as they did if the FASB had not sanctioned smoothing mechanisms and buried the return on plan assets in operating income.

I believe the FASB needs to address the issue of who should do the smoothing from a conceptual basis. Should the accountant do the smoothing based on accounting rules? Should the rules provide for smoothing of the nonrecurring items over an economic cycle? Or should the job of smoothing, or normalizing earnings, be left for analysts? Should it be up to analysts to identify an unusual event or one that will not recur every period with certainty and then pull it out and treat it differently in valuation? My personal view is that smoothing is the job of analysts. Accountants should be reporting exactly what happened in the period. It is the analysts' job to interpret and then use that interpretation to derive a valuation.

Conclusion

The financial reporting changes of the past 30 years have led progressively toward more and more information and tools for the analyst. But the increase in the quality of financial reporting has led to questions about the reporting and treatment of pension expense, employee stock options, and derivatives, all of which are related to earnings quality. The move from a principle-based system to a rule-based system opened the door to a multitude of exceptions to the rules and led to a corresponding abundance of guidelines to direct the implementation of the rules (such as SFAS No. 133, for example, which has more than 1,000 pages of guidance). The resolution of today's emerging issues, such as revenue recognition, financial statement disclosure, and smoothing, will have a tremendous impact on the information that will be available to analysts in the future and thus will affect valuation. Just as the decisions of the Trueblood and Wheat Committees created the current state of financial reporting, the decisions made in trying to resolve today's issues will determine the course of financial reporting in the future.

Question and Answer Session

Patricia A. McConnell

Question: What changes ought to be made to the accounting standards for barter transactions?

McConnell: Barter transactions are a difficult issue to address. The accounting standard on barter transactions (referred to technically as nonmonetary exchanges) is based on a sound principle—that is, transactions should be recorded at the fair value of the goods and services exchanged. If one of the goods and services isn't cash, you have to determine the fair value of the goods and services exchanged.

Barter transactions would not have received so much publicity in the late 1990s if the financial markets hadn't been valuing companies based on revenue. Companies entered into barter transactions that didn't produce any gains or losses simply because the transaction produced revenue. Thus, they could improve their valuations.

To address some of the abuses, the FASB issued a rule that says revenue on a barter transaction cannot be booked unless similar transactions have taken place for cash. But it doesn't take a financial genius to determine how to game that rule. Swapping goods and services is not necessary. This led to the emergence of what the SEC staff refers to as "round-trip transactions." I buy advertising from you and pay you $100 million, and you buy envelopes from me and pay me $100 million. We both need the product the other is selling, so the transaction appears to have economic substance. We both have $100 million in revenue, and it was a cash transaction.

No neat solution exists for regulating barter transactions. At the end of the day, the key question is: Was there really an economic business purpose for the transaction? If the answer is no, then whether cash or goods and services exchanged hands does not matter; if the transaction had no economic basis, it should not be considered revenue. In many cases, however, you need a crystal ball to determine whether any real economic purpose accompanied the exchange.

Question: In regard to revenue recognition, instances of "channel stuffing" keep recurring. Do we need new rules?

McConnell: In my view, "channel stuffing" (effectively saying, with a wink and a nod, "Take more inventory than you really need; you can send it back if you don't sell it") is an issue of earnings quality. So, I don't think we need new rules. In fact, the only rule that I can think of proposing to address this problem is a rule that forbids the use of sales incentives.

Basically, channel stuffing is stealing sales from future periods and booking them in the current period. The practice is often more blatant than a wink and a nod, such as offering a deep discount on the next purchase if the buyer will take delivery in the current period at the regular price or telling the buyer to stock up now because prices are going up. Analysts who value companies based on revenues will get taken in by this practice. Again, analysts must understand the company's business, determine how the company is making its sales, and talk to the distributors to find out why they're buying more of the product than expected, given the economic cycle. Analysts must find out if the company offered a big discount or threatened price increases, which would lower next-period sales and would certainly affect company earnings. The channel-stuffing issues weren't nearly as great a problem until the market started valuing companies based on revenues rather than earnings.

Question: Are accounting scandals simply a lagging economic indicator, or are they driven by a different dynamic?

McConnell: I think they are a lagging economic indicator. Good times lead to excesses. When the markets rose in the late 1990s, I felt sorry for the fundamental analysts, who spent their days crunching numbers to value a company only to have it sell at multiples of their estimates. In the search for culprits, no one is without blame; one of the things forgotten was the underlying rule of investments—the risk–reward trade-off. So, when the rewards were getting staggeringly high, we should've realized the amount of risk involved.

Question: Will the stock market's recovery be more difficult in 2003 as analysts begin to reduce EPS estimates because of pension and option accounting adjustments? Will the markets be negatively influenced by purely cosmetic accounting changes?

McConnell: I don't think the market is taken in by pure accounting adjustments when it understands the adjustments and what is driving them. But that requires two caveats: for the information to be available and for someone to read it.

And I would make a distinction between the stock compensation adjustment and the pension adjustment. The employee stock option adjustment is a cash adjustment, which is difficult for most people to believe because there is no cash inflow or outflow at the date the option is granted. In other words, no cash runs through the company's bank accounts. But analytically, the transaction is an operating cash outflow and a financing cash inflow. The company paid its employees, and the employees "bought" options from the company. In valuation, the distinction between an operating cash flow and a financing cash flow is critically important. Granted, the option adjustment has no effect on the company's cash balance, but that is because two different economic transactions are occurring that net to zero.

The pension accounting adjustment issue is slightly different. The cash flow is the contribution that the company makes to its pension plan, and that does not, in any rational way, match the accounting for pension plan expense. What has confused the markets is that the FASB, as I said earlier, provided a mechanism in pension accounting to smooth out the peaks and valleys of the effects of market movements and interest rate changes on net pension cost or income. During the bull market of the 1990s, companies earned huge returns on plan assets, which offset the other components of net pension cost. As a result, the returns were buried in operating income. Because the pension accounting standard was relatively new (it came out in 1987) and was enormously complicated, many market participants never untangled the reality behind the accounting. So, the result was a stock-market-linked return embedded in operating income to which analysts were applying the company's regular multiple, the multiple for earnings derived from sales of its product or service.

As the investment management business exploded in the late 1990s, more people entered the investment community who had learned about pension accounting. These investors and analysts recognized that earnings quality was poor because of pension accounting and that the multiple placed on many of these companies was too high because most of their earnings were coming from the return on their plan assets.

In a down cycle, when company earnings are depressed because of the stock-market-linked returns on pension assets, those earnings are just as poor in quality as the up-market earnings were in the 1990s. I hope that the market doesn't compound the mistake of the 1990s and put a normal multiple on the negative stock market returns that will be impacting net pension expense over the next couple of years. Doing so would simply compound the errors made in the 1990s.

Question: Do Bear Stearns analysts' EPS forecasts incorporate pension and stock option effects?

McConnell: They're supposed to incorporate pension and stock option effects. In fact, my group recently held a seminar to answer our analysts' questions about how to estimate employee stock compensation expense going forward, and we've been working with them for a decade on the pension issues.

Appendix A.

Summary of SFAS No. 87
Employers' Accounting for Pensions (Issued 12/85)

Summary

This Statement supersedes previous standards for employers' accounting for pensions. The most significant changes to past practice affect an employer's accounting for a single-employer defined benefit pension plan, although some provisions also apply to an employer that participates in a multiemployer plan or sponsors a defined contribution plan.

Measuring cost and reporting liabilities resulting from defined benefit pension plans have been sources of accounting controversy for many years. Both the Committee on Accounting Procedure, in 1956, and the Accounting Principles Board (APB), in 1966, concluded that improvements in pension accounting were necessary beyond what was considered practical at those times.

After 1966, the importance of information about pensions grew with increases in the number of plans and amounts of pension assets and obligations. There were significant changes in both the legal environment (for example, the enactment of ERISA) and the economic environment (for example, higher inflation and interest rates). Critics of prior accounting requirements, including users of financial statements, became aware that reported pension cost was not comparable from one company to another and often was not consistent from period to period for the same company. They also became aware that significant pension-related obligations and assets were not recognized in financial statements.

Funding and Accrual Accounting

This Statement reaffirms the usefulness of information based on accrual accounting. Accrual accounting goes beyond cash transactions to provide information about assets, liabilities, and earnings. The Board has concluded, as did the APB in 1966, that net pension cost for a period is not necessarily determined by the amount the employer decides to contribute to the plan for that period. Many factors (including tax considerations and availability of both cash and alternative investment opportunities) that affect funding decisions should not be allowed to dictate accounting results if the accounting is to provide the most useful information.

The conclusion that accounting information on an accrual basis is needed does not mean that accounting information and funding decisions are unrelated. In pensions, as in other areas, managers may use accounting information along with other factors in making financial decisions. Some employers may decide to change their pension funding policies based in part on the new accounting information. Financial statements should provide information that is useful to those who make economic decisions, and the decision to fund a pension plan to a greater or lesser extent is an economic decision. The Board, however, does not have as an objective either an increase or a decrease in the funding level of any particular plan or plans. Neither does the Board believe that the information required by this Statement is the only information needed to make a funding decision or that net periodic pension cost, as defined, is necessarily the appropriate amount for any particular employer's periodic contribution.

Fundamentals of Pension Accounting

In applying accrual accounting to pensions, this Statement retains three fundamental aspects of past pension accounting: *delaying recognition* of certain events, reporting *net cost*, and *offsetting* liabilities and assets. Those three features of practice have shaped financial reporting for pensions for many years, although they have been neither explicitly addressed nor widely understood, and they conflict in some respects with accounting principles applied elsewhere. The *delayed recognition* feature means that changes in the pension obligation (including those resulting from plan amendments) and changes in the value of assets set aside to meet those obligations are not recognized as they occur but are recognized systematically and gradually over subsequent periods. All changes are ultimately recognized except to the extent they may be offset by subsequent changes, but at any point changes that have been identified and

---

[1] The summary pages of these statements, copyright by Financial Accounting Standards Board, 401 Merritt 7, P.O. Box 5116, Norwalk, Connecticut 06856-5116, USA, are reprinted with permission. Complete copies of these documents are available from the FASB.

quantified await subsequent accounting recognition as net cost components and as liabilities or assets.

The *net cost* feature means that the recognized consequences of events and transactions affecting a pension plan are reported as a single net amount in the employer's financial statements. That approach aggregates at least three items that might be reported separately for any other part of an employer's operations: the compensation cost of benefits promised, interest cost resulting from deferred payment of those benefits, and the results of investing what are often significant amounts of assets.

The *offsetting* feature means that recognized values of assets contributed to a plan and liabilities for pensions recognized as net pension cost of past periods are shown net in the employer's statement of financial position, even though the liability has not been settled, the assets may be still largely controlled, and substantial risks and rewards associated with both of those amounts are clearly borne by the employer.

Within those three features of practice that are retained by this Statement, the Board has sought to achieve more useful financial reporting through three changes:

a. This Statement requires a standardized method for measuring net periodic pension cost that is intended to improve comparability and understandability by recognizing the compensation cost of an employee's pension over that employee's approximate service period and by relating that cost more directly to the terms of the plan.
b. This Statement requires immediate recognition of a liability (the minimum liability) when the accumulated benefit obligation exceeds the fair value of plan assets, although it continues to delay recognition of the offsetting amount as an increase in net periodic pension cost.
c. This Statement requires expanded disclosures intended to provide more complete and more current information than can be practically incorporated in financial statements at the present time.

Cost Recognition and Measurement

A fundamental objective of this Statement is to recognize the compensation cost of an employee's pension benefits (including prior service cost) over that employee's approximate service period. Many respondents to *Preliminary Views* and the Exposure Draft on employers' accounting for pensions agreed with that objective, which conflicts with some aspects of past practice under APB Opinion No. 8, *Accounting for the Cost of Pension Plans.*

The Board believes that the understandability, comparability, and usefulness of pension information will be improved by narrowing the past range of methods for allocating or attributing the cost of an employee's pension to individual periods of service. The Board was unable to identify differences in circumstances that would make it appropriate for different employers to use fundamentally different accounting methods or for a single employer to use different methods for different plans.

The Board believes that the terms of the plan that define the benefits an employee will receive (the plan's benefit formula) provide the most relevant and reliable indication of how pension cost and pension obligations are incurred. In the absence of convincing evidence that the substance of an exchange is different from that indicated by the agreement between the parties, accounting has traditionally looked to the terms of the agreement as a basis for recording the exchange. Unlike some other methods previously used for pension accounting, the method required by this Statement focuses more directly on the plan's benefit formula as the basis for determining the benefit earned, and therefore the cost incurred, in each individual period.

Statement of Financial Position

The Board believes that this Statement represents an improvement in past practices for the reporting of financial position in two ways. First, recognition of the cost of pensions over employees' service periods will result in earlier (but still gradual) recognition of significant liabilities that were reflected more slowly in the past financial statements of some employers. Second, the requirement to recognize a minimum liability limits the extent to which the delayed recognition of plan amendments and losses in net periodic pension cost can result in omission of certain liabilities from statements of financial position.

Recognition of a measure of at least the minimum pension obligation as a liability is not a new idea. Accounting Research Bulletin No. 47, *Accounting for Costs of Pension Plans,* published in 1956, stated that "as a minimum, the accounts and financial statements should reflect accruals which equal the present worth, actuarially calculated, of pension commitments to employees to the extent that pension rights have vested in the employees, reduced, in the case of the balance sheet, by any accumulated trusteed funds or annuity contracts purchased." Opinion 8 required that "if the company has a legal obligation for pension cost in excess of amounts paid or accrued, the excess should be shown in the balance sheet as both a liability and a deferred charge."

The Board believes that an employer with an unfunded pension obligation has a liability and an employer with an overfunded pension obligation has an asset. The most relevant and reliable information available about that liability or asset is based on the fair value of plan assets and a measure of the present value of the obligation using current, explicit assumptions. The Board concluded, however, that recognition in financial statements of those amounts in their entirety would be too great a change from past practice. Some Board members were also influenced by concerns about the reliability of measures of the obligation.

The delayed recognition included in this Statement results in excluding the most current and most relevant information from the statement of financial position. That information, however, is included in the required disclosures.

Information Needed

The Board believes that users of financial reports need information beyond that previously disclosed to be able to assess the status of an employer's pension arrangements and their effects on the employer's financial position and results of operations. Most respondents agreed, and this Statement requires certain disclosures not previously required.

This Statement requires disclosure of the components of net pension cost and of the projected benefit obligation. One of the factors that has made pension information difficult to understand is that past practice and terminology combined elements that are different in substance and effect into net amounts. Although the Board agreed to retain from past pension accounting practice the basic features of reporting net cost and offsetting liabilities and assets, the Board believes that disclosure of the components will significantly assist users in understanding the economic events that have occurred. Those disclosures also make it easier to understand why reported amounts change from period to period, especially when a large cost or asset is offset by a large revenue or liability to produce a relatively small net reported amount.

* * * * *

After considering the range of comments on *Preliminary Views* and the Exposure Draft, the Board concluded that this Statement represents a worthwhile improvement in financial reporting. Opinion 8 noted in 1966 that "accounting for pension cost is in a transitional stage." The Board believes that is still true in 1985. FASB Concepts Statement No. 5, *Recognition and Measurement in Financial Statements of Business Enterprises,* paragraph 2, indicates that "the Board intends future change [in practice] to occur in the gradual, evolutionary way that has characterized past change."

Appendix B.

Summary of SFAS No. 123
Accounting for Stock-Based Compensation (Issued 10/95)

Summary

This Statement establishes financial accounting and reporting standards for stockbased employee compensation plans. Those plans include all arrangements by which employees receive shares of stock or other equity instruments of the employer or the employer incurs liabilities to employees in amounts based on the price of the employer's stock. Examples are stock purchase plans, stock options, restricted stock, and stock appreciation rights.

This Statement also applies to transactions in which an entity issues its equity instruments to acquire goods or services from nonemployees. Those transactions must be accounted for based on the fair value of the consideration received or the fair value of the equity instruments issued, whichever is more reliably measurable.

Accounting for Awards of Stock-Based Compensation to Employees

This Statement defines a *fair value based method* of accounting for an employee stock option or similar equity instrument and encourages all entities to adopt that method of accounting for all of their employee stock compensation plans. However, it also allows an entity to continue to measure compensation cost for those plans using the *intrinsic value based method* of accounting prescribed by APB Opinion No. 25, *Accounting for Stock Issued to Employees*. The fair value based method is preferable to the Opinion 25 method for purposes of justifying a change in accounting principle under APB Opinion No. 20, *Accounting Changes*. Entities electing to remain with the accounting in Opinion 25 must make pro forma disclosures of net income and, if presented, earnings per share, as if the fair value based method of accounting defined in this Statement had been applied.

Under the fair value based method, compensation cost is measured at the grant date based on the value of the award and is recognized over the service period, which is usually the vesting period. Under the intrinsic value based method, compensation cost is the excess, if any, of the quoted market price of the stock at grant date or other measurement date over the amount an employee must pay to acquire the stock. Most fixed stock option plans—the most common type of stock compensation plan—have no intrinsic value at grant date, and under Opinion 25 no compensation cost is recognized for them. Compensation cost is recognized for other types of stock-based compensation plans under Opinion 25, including plans with variable, usually performance-based, features.

Stock Compensation Awards Required to Be Settled by Issuing Equity Instruments Stock Options

For stock options, fair value is determined using an option-pricing model that takes into account the stock price at the grant date, the exercise price, the expected life of the option, the volatility of the underlying stock and the expected dividends on it, and the riskfree interest rate over the expected life of the option. Nonpublic entities are permitted to exclude the volatility factor in estimating the value of their stock options, which results in measurement at *minimum value*. The fair value of an option estimated at the grant date is not subsequently adjusted for changes in the price of the underlying stock or its volatility, the life of the option, dividends on the stock, or the risk-free interest rate.

Nonvested Stock

The fair value of a share of nonvested stock (usually referred to as restricted stock) awarded to an employee is measured at the market price of a share of a nonrestricted stock on the grant date unless a restriction will be imposed after the employee has a vested right to it, in which case fair value is estimated taking that restriction into account.

Employee Stock Purchase Plans

An employee stock purchase plan that allows employees to purchase stock at a discount from market price is not compensatory if it satisfies three conditions: (a) the discount is relatively small (5 percent or less satisfies this condition automatically, though in some cases a greater discount also might be justified as noncompensatory), (b) substantially all full-time employees may participate on an equitable basis, and (c) the plan incorporates no option features such as allowing the employee to purchase the stock at a fixed discount from the lesser of the market price at grant date or date of purchase.

Stock Compensation Awards Required to Be Settled by Paying Cash

Some stock-based compensation plans require an employer to pay an employee, either on demand or at a specified date, a cash amount determined by the increase in the employer's stock price from a specified level. The entity must measure compensation cost for that award in the amount of the changes in the stock price in the periods in which the changes occur.

Disclosures

This Statement requires that an employer's financial statements include certain disclosures about stock-based employee compensation arrangements regardless of the method used to account for them.

The pro forma amounts required to be disclosed by an employer that continues to apply the accounting provisions of Opinion 25 will reflect the difference between compensation cost, if any, included in net income and the related cost measured by the fair value based method defined in this Statement, including tax effects, if any, that would have been recognized in the income statement if the fair value based method had been used. The required pro forma amounts will not reflect any other adjustments to reported net income or, if presented, earnings per share.

Effective Date and Transition

The accounting requirements of this Statement are effective for transactions entered into in fiscal years that begin after December 15, 1995, though they may be adopted on issuance.

The disclosure requirements of this Statement are effective for financial statements for fiscal years beginning after December 15, 1995, or for an earlier fiscal year for which this Statement is initially adopted for recognizing compensation cost. Pro forma disclosures required for entities that elect to continue to measure compensation cost using Opinion 25 must include the effects of all awards granted in fiscal years that begin after December 15, 1994. Pro forma disclosures for awards granted in the first fiscal year beginning after December 15, 1994, need not be included in financial statements for that fiscal year but should be presented subsequently whenever financial statements for that fiscal year are presented for comparative purposes with financial statements for a later fiscal year.

Appendix C.

Summary of SFAS No. 133
Accounting for Derivative Instruments and Hedging Activities (Issued 6/98)

Summary

This Statement establishes accounting and reporting standards for derivative instruments, including certain derivative instruments embedded in other contracts, (collectively referred to as derivatives) and for hedging activities. It requires that an entity recognize all derivatives as either assets or liabilities in the statement of financial position and measure those instruments at fair value. If certain conditions are met, a derivative may be specifically designated as (a) a hedge of the exposure to changes in the fair value of a recognized asset or liability or an unrecognized firm commitment, (b) a hedge of the exposure to variable cash flows of a forecasted transaction, or (c) a hedge of the foreign currency exposure of a net investment in a foreign operation, an unrecognized firm commitment, an available-for-sale security, or a foreign-currency-denominated forecasted transaction.

The accounting for changes in the fair value of a derivative (that is, gains and losses) depends on the intended use of the derivative and the resulting designation.

- For a derivative designated as hedging the exposure to changes in the fair value of a recognized asset or liability or a firm commitment (referred to as a fair value hedge), the gain or loss is recognized in earnings in the period of change together with the offsetting loss or gain on the hedged item attributable to the risk being hedged. The effect of that accounting is to reflect in earnings the extent to which the hedge is not effective in achieving offsetting changes in fair value.
- For a derivative designated as hedging the exposure to variable cash flows of a forecasted transaction (referred to as a cash flow hedge), the effective portion of the derivative's gain or loss is initially reported as a component of other comprehensive income (outside earnings) and subsequently reclassified into earnings when the forecasted transaction affects earnings. The ineffective portion of the gain or loss is reported in earnings immediately.
- For a derivative designated as hedging the foreign currency exposure of a net investment in a foreign operation, the gain or loss is reported in other comprehensive income (outside earnings) as part of the cumulative translation adjustment. The accounting for a fair value hedge described above applies to a derivative designated as a hedge of the foreign currency exposure of an unrecognized firm commitment or an available-for-sale security. Similarly, the accounting for a cash flow hedge described above applies to a derivative designated as a hedge of the foreign currency exposure of a foreign-currency-denominated forecasted transaction.
- For a derivative not designated as a hedging instrument, the gain or loss is recognized in earnings in the period of change.

Under this Statement, an entity that elects to apply hedge accounting is required to establish at the inception of the hedge the method it will use for assessing the effectiveness of the hedging derivative and the measurement approach for determining the ineffective aspect of the hedge. Those methods must be consistent with the entity's approach to managing risk.

This Statement applies to all entities. A not-for-profit organization should recognize the change in fair value of all derivatives as a change in net assets in the period of change. In a fair value hedge, the changes in the fair value of the hedged item attributable to the risk being hedged also are recognized. However, because of the format of their statement of financial performance, not-for-profit organizations are not permitted special hedge accounting for derivatives used to hedge forecasted transactions. This Statement does not address how a not-for-profit organization should determine the components of an operating measure if one is presented.

This Statement precludes designating a nonderivative financial instrument as a hedge of an asset, liability, unrecognized firm commitment, or forecasted transaction except that a nonderivative instrument denominated in a foreign currency may be designated as a hedge of the foreign currency exposure of an unrecognized firm commitment denominated in a foreign currency or a net investment in a foreign operation.

This Statement amends FASB Statement No. 52, *Foreign Currency Translation*, to permit special accounting for a hedge of a foreign currency forecasted transaction with a derivative. It supersedes

FASB Statements No. 80, *Accounting for Futures Contracts*, No. 105, *Disclosure of Information about Financial Instruments with Off-Balance-Sheet Risk and Financial Instruments with Concentrations of Credit Risk*, and No. 119, *Disclosure about Derivative Financial Instruments and Fair Value of Financial Instruments.* It amends FASB Statement No. 107, *Disclosures about Fair Value of Financial Instruments,* to include in Statement 107 the disclosure provisions about concentrations of credit risk from Statement 105. This Statement also nullifies or modifies the consensuses reached in a number of issues addressed by the Emerging Issues Task Force.

This Statement is effective for all fiscal quarters of fiscal years beginning after June 15, 1999. Initial application of this Statement should be as of the beginning of an entity's fiscal quarter; on that date, hedging relationships must be designated anew and documented pursuant to the provisions of this Statement. Earlier application of all of the provisions of this Statement is encouraged, but it is permitted only as of the beginning of any fiscal quarter that begins after issuance of this Statement. This Statement should not be applied retroactively to financial statements of prior periods.

Appendix D.

Summary of SFAS No. 141
Business Combinations (Issued 6/01)

Summary

This Statement addresses financial accounting and reporting for business combinations and supersedes APB Opinion No. 16, *Business Combinations,* and FASB Statement No. 38, *Accounting for Preacquisition Contingencies of Purchased Enterprises.* All business combinations in the scope of this Statement are to be accounted for using one method, the purchase method.

Reasons for Issuing This Statement

Under Opinion 16, business combinations were accounted for using one of two methods, the pooling-of-interests method (pooling method) or the purchase method. Use of the pooling method was required whenever 12 criteria were met; otherwise, the purchase method was to be used. Because those 12 criteria did not distinguish economically dissimilar transactions, similar business combinations were accounted for using different methods that produced dramatically different financial statement results. Consequently:

- Analysts and other users of financial statements indicated that it was difficult to compare the financial results of entities because different methods of accounting for business combinations were used.
- Users of financial statements also indicated a need for better information about intangible assets because those assets are an increasingly important economic resource for many entities and are an increasing proportion of the assets acquired in many business combinations. While the purchase method recognizes all intangible assets acquired in a business combination (either separately or as goodwill), only those intangible assets previously recorded by the acquired entity are recognized when the pooling method is used.
- Company managements indicated that the differences between the pooling and purchase methods of accounting for business combinations affected competition in markets for mergers and acquisitions.

Differences between This Statement and Opinion 16

The provisions of this Statement reflect a fundamentally different approach to accounting for business combinations than was taken in Opinion 16. The single-method approach used in this Statement reflects the conclusion that virtually all business combinations are acquisitions and, thus, all business combinations should be accounted for in the same way that other asset acquisitions are accounted for—based on the values exchanged.

This Statement changes the accounting for business combinations in Opinion 16 in the following significant respects:

- This Statement requires that all business combinations be accounted for by a single method—the purchase method.
- In contrast to Opinion 16, which required separate recognition of intangible assets that can be identified and named, this Statement requires that they be recognized as assets apart from goodwill if they meet one of two criteria—the contractual-legal criterion or the separability criterion. To assist in identifying acquired intangible assets, this Statement also provides an illustrative list of intangible assets that meet either of those criteria.
- In addition to the disclosure requirements in Opinion 16, this Statement requires disclosure of the primary reasons for a business combination and the allocation of the purchase price paid to the assets acquired and liabilities assumed by major balance sheet caption. When the amounts of goodwill and intangible assets acquired are significant in relation to the purchase price paid, disclosure of other information about those assets is required, such as the amount of goodwill by reportable segment and the amount of the purchase price assigned to each major intangible asset class.

This Statement does not change many of the provisions of Opinion 16 and Statement 38 related to the application of the purchase method. For example, this Statement does not fundamentally change the guidance for determining the cost of an acquired entity and allocating that cost to the assets acquired and liabilities assumed, the accounting for contingent consideration, and the accounting for preacquisition contingencies. That guidance is carried forward in this Statement (but was not reconsidered by the Board). Also, this Statement does not change the requirement to write off certain research and development assets acquired in a business combination as required by FASB Interpretation No. 4, *Applicability of FASB Statement No. 2 to Business Combinations Accounted for by the Purchase Method.*

How the Changes in This Statement Improve Financial Reporting

The changes to accounting for business combinations required by this Statement improve financial reporting because the financial statements of entities that engage in business combinations will better reflect the underlying economics of those transactions. In particular, application of this Statement will result in financial statements that:

- *Better reflect the investment made in an acquired entity*—the purchase method records a business combination based on the values exchanged, thus users are provided information about the total purchase price paid to acquire another entity, which allows for more meaningful evaluation of the subsequent performance of that investment. Similar information is not provided when the pooling method is used.
- *Improve the comparability of reported financial information*—all business combinations are accounted for using a single method, thus, users are able to compare the financial results of entities that engage in business combinations on an apples-to-apples basis. That is because the assets acquired and liabilities assumed in all business combinations are recognized and measured in the same way regardless of the nature of the consideration exchanged for them.
- *Provide more complete financial information*—the explicit criteria for recognition of intangible assets apart from goodwill and the expanded disclosure requirements of this Statement provide more information about the assets acquired and liabilities assumed in business combinations. That additional information should, among other things, provide users with a better understanding of the resources acquired and improve their ability to assess future profitability and cash flows.

Requiring one method of accounting reduces the costs of accounting for business combinations. For example, it eliminates the costs incurred by entities in positioning themselves to meet the criteria for using the pooling method, such as the monetary and nonmonetary costs of taking actions they might not otherwise have taken or refraining from actions they might otherwise have taken.

How the Conclusions in This Statement Relate to the Conceptual Framework

The Board concluded that because virtually all business combinations are acquisitions, requiring one method of accounting for economically similar transactions is consistent with the concepts of representational faithfulness and comparability as discussed in FASB Concepts Statement No. 2, *Qualitative Characteristics of Accounting Information.* In developing this Statement, the Board also concluded that goodwill should be recognized as an asset because it meets the assets definition in FASB Concepts Statement No. 6, *Elements of Financial Statements,* and the asset recognition criteria in FASB Concepts Statement No. 5, *Recognition and Measurement in Financial Statements of Business Enterprises.*

The Board also noted that FASB Concepts Statement No. 1, *Objectives of Financial Reporting by Business Enterprises,* states that financial reporting should provide information that helps in assessing the amounts, timing, and uncertainty of prospective net cash inflows to an entity. The Board noted that because the purchase method records the net assets acquired in a business combination at their fair values, the information provided by that method is more useful in assessing the cash-generating abilities of the net assets acquired than the information provided by the pooling method.

Some of the Board's constituents indicated that the pooling method should be retained for public policy reasons. For example, some argued that eliminating the pooling method would impede consolidation of certain industries, reduce the amount of capital flowing into certain industries, and slow the development of new technology. Concepts Statement 2 states that a necessary and important characteristic of accounting information is neutrality. In the context of business combinations, neutrality means that the accounting standards should neither encourage nor discourage business combinations but rather, provide information about those combinations that is fair and evenhanded. The Board concluded that its public policy goal is to issue accounting standards that result in neutral and representationally faithful financial information and that eliminating the pooling method is consistent with that goal.

The Effective Date of This Statement

The provisions of this Statement apply to all business combinations initiated after June 30, 2001. This Statement also applies to all business combinations accounted for using the purchase method for which the date of acquisition is July 1, 2001, or later.

This Statement does not apply, however, to combinations of two or more not-for-profit organizations, the acquisition of a for-profit business entity by a not-for-profit organization, and combinations of two or more mutual enterprises.

Appendix E.
Summary of SFAS No. 142
Goodwill and Other Intangible Assets (Issued 6/01)

Summary

This Statement addresses financial accounting and reporting for acquired goodwill and other intangible assets and supersedes APB Opinion No. 17, *Intangible Assets*. It addresses how intangible assets that are acquired individually or with a group of other assets (but not those acquired in a business combination) should be accounted for in financial statements upon their acquisition. This Statement also addresses how goodwill and other intangible assets should be accounted for after they have been initially recognized in the financial statements.

Reasons for Issuing This Statement

Analysts and other users of financial statements, as well as company managements, noted that intangible assets are an increasingly important economic resource for many entities and are an increasing proportion of the assets acquired in many transactions. As a result, better information about intangible assets was needed. Financial statement users also indicated that they did not regard goodwill amortization expense as being useful information in analyzing investments.

Differences between This Statement and Opinion 17

This Statement changes the unit of account for goodwill and takes a very different approach to how goodwill and other intangible assets are accounted for subsequent to their initial recognition. Because goodwill and some intangible assets will no longer be amortized, the reported amounts of goodwill and intangible assets (as well as total assets) will not decrease at the same time and in the same manner as under previous standards. There may be more volatility in reported income than under previous standards because impairment losses are likely to occur irregularly and in varying amounts.

This Statement changes the subsequent accounting for goodwill and other intangible assets in the following significant respects:

- Acquiring entities usually integrate acquired entities into their operations, and thus the acquirers' expectations of benefits from the resulting synergies usually are reflected in the premium that they pay to acquire those entities. However, the transaction-based approach to accounting for goodwill under Opinion 17 treated the acquired entity as if it remained a stand-alone entity rather than being integrated with the acquiring entity; as a result, the portion of the premium related to expected synergies (goodwill) was not accounted for appropriately. This Statement adopts a more aggregate view of goodwill and bases the accounting for goodwill on the units of the combined entity into which an acquired entity is integrated (those units are referred to as reporting units).

- Opinion 17 presumed that goodwill and all other intangible assets were wasting assets (that is, finite lived), and thus the amounts assigned to them should be amortized in determining net income; Opinion 17 also mandated an arbitrary ceiling of 40 years for that amortization. This Statement does not presume that those assets are wasting assets. Instead, goodwill and intangible assets that have indefinite useful lives will not be amortized but rather will be tested at least annually for impairment. Intangible assets that have finite useful lives will continue to be amortized over their useful lives, but without the constraint of an arbitrary ceiling.

- Previous standards provided little guidance about how to determine and measure goodwill impairment; as a result, the accounting for goodwill impairments was not consistent and not comparable and yielded information of questionable usefulness. This Statement provides specific guidance for testing goodwill for impairment. Goodwill will be tested for impairment at least annually using a two-step process that begins with an estimation of the fair value of a reporting unit. The first step is a screen for potential impairment, and the second step measures the amount of impairment, if any. However, if certain criteria are met, the requirement to test goodwill for impairment annually can be satisfied without a remeasurement of the fair value of a reporting unit.

- In addition, this Statement provides specific guidance on testing intangible assets that will not be amortized for impairment and thus removes

those intangible assets from the scope of other impairment guidance. Intangible assets that are not amortized will be tested for impairment at least annually by comparing the fair values of those assets with their recorded amounts.
- This Statement requires disclosure of information about goodwill and other intangible assets in the years subsequent to their acquisition that was not previously required. Required disclosures include information about the changes in the carrying amount of goodwill from period to period (in the aggregate and by reportable segment), the carrying amount of intangible assets by major intangible asset class for those assets subject to amortization and for those not subject to amortization, and the estimated intangible asset amortization expense for the next five years.

This Statement carries forward without reconsideration the provisions of Opinion 17 related to the accounting for internally developed intangible assets. This Statement also does not change the requirement to expense the cost of certain acquired research and development assets at the date of acquisition as required by FASB Statement No. 2, *Accounting for Research and Development Costs*, and FASB Interpretation No. 4, *Applicability of FASB Statement No. 2 to Business Combinations Accounted for by the Purchase Method*.

How the Changes in This Statement Improve Financial Reporting

The changes included in this Statement will improve financial reporting because the financial statements of entities that acquire goodwill and other intangible assets will better reflect the underlying economics of those assets. As a result, financial statement users will be better able to understand the investments made in those assets and the subsequent performance of those investments. The enhanced disclosures about goodwill and intangible assets subsequent to their acquisition also will provide users with a better understanding of the expectations about and changes in those assets over time, thereby improving their ability to assess future profitability and cash flows.

How the Conclusions in This Statement Relate to the Conceptual Framework

The Board concluded that amortization of goodwill was not consistent with the concept of representational faithfulness, as discussed in FASB Concepts Statement No. 2, *Qualitative Characteristics of Accounting Information*. The Board concluded that nonamortization of goodwill coupled with impairment testing *is* consistent with that concept. The appropriate balance of both relevance and reliability and costs and benefits also was central to the Board's conclusion that this Statement will improve financial reporting.

This Statement utilizes the guidance in FASB Concepts Statement No. 7, *Using Cash Flow Information and Present Value in Accounting Measurements*, for estimating the fair values used in testing both goodwill and other intangible assets that are not being amortized for impairment.

The Effective Date of This Statement

The provisions of this Statement are required to be applied starting with fiscal years beginning after December 15, 2001. Early application is permitted for entities with fiscal years beginning after March 15, 2001, provided that the first interim financial statements have not previously been issued. This Statement is required to be applied at the beginning of an entity's fiscal year and to be applied to all goodwill and other intangible assets recognized in its financial statements at that date. Impairment losses for goodwill and indefinite-lived intangible assets that arise due to the initial application of this Statement (resulting from a transitional impairment test) are to be reported as resulting from a change in accounting principle.

There are two exceptions to the date at which this Statement becomes effective:
- Goodwill and intangible assets acquired after June 30, 2001, will be subject immediately to the nonamortization and amortization provisions of this Statement.
- The provisions of this Statement will not be applicable to goodwill and other intangible assets arising from combinations between mutual enterprises or to not-for-profit organizations until the Board completes its deliberations with respect to application of the purchase method by those entities.

U.S. POSTAL SERVICE
STATEMENT OF OWNERSHIP, MANAGEMENT, AND CIRCULATION
(Required by 39 U.S.C. 3685)

1. Title of Publication: *AIMR Continuing Education*
2. Publication No.: 013-739
3. Filing Date: November 11, 2002
4. Issue Frequency: Four Times a Year
5. Number of Issues Published Annually: 4
6. Annual Subscription Price: US$100
7. Complete Mailing Address of Known Office of Publication (Street, City, County, State, and Zip+4) (Not Printer)
   Association for Investment Management and Research
   P.O. Box 3668, Charlottesville, VA 22903-0668
8. Complete Mailing Address of Headquarters or General Business Office of Publisher (Not Printer)
   Association for Investment Management and Research
   P.O. Box 3668, Charlottesville, VA 22903-0668
9. Full Names and Complete Mailing Addresses of Publisher, Editor, and Managing Editor (Do Not Leave Blank)
   Publisher (Name and Complete Mailing Address)
     AIMR, P.O. Box 3668, Charlottesville, VA 22903-0668
   Editor (Name and Complete Mailing Address)
     Kathryn D. Jost, AIMR, P.O. Box 3668, Charlottesville, VA 22903-0668
   Managing Editor (Name and Complete Mailing Address)
     Jaynee M. Dudley, AIMR, P.O. Box 3668, Charlottesville, VA 22903-0688
10. Owner (If owned by a corporation, its name and address must be stated and also immediately thereafter the names and addresses of stockholders owning or holding 1 percent or more of the total amount of stock. If not owned by a corporation, the names and addresses of the individual owners must be given. If owned by a partnership or other unincorporated firm, its name and address as well as that of each individual must be given. If the publication is published by a nonprofit organization, its name and address must be given.) (Do Not Leave Blank)
    Association for Investment Management and Research, P.O. Box 3668, Charlottesville, VA 22903-0668
11. Known Bondholders, Mortgagees, and Other Security Holders Owning or Holding 1 Percent or More of Total Amount of Bonds, Mortgages or Other Securities. If none, check here. ✔ None.
12. For completion by nonprofit organization authorized to mail at special rates. The purpose, function, and nonprofit status of the organization and the exempt status for Federal income tax purposes: (Check one.)

    ✔ Has Not Changed During Preceding 12 Months
    ☐ Has Changed During Preceding 12 Months (If changed, publisher must submit explanation of change with this statement.)

13. Publication Name: *AIMR Continuing Education*
14. Issue Date for Circulation Data Below: January through November 2002

15. Extent and Nature of Circulation	Average No. Copies Each Issue During Preceding 12 Months	Actual No. of Copies of Single Issue Published Nearest to Filing Date
a. Total No. Copies (Net Press Run)	52,790	51,478
b. Paid and/or Requested Circulation		
1. Sales Through Dealers and Carriers, Street Vendors, and Counter Sales		
2. Paid or Requested Mail Subscriptions	46,289	47,741
c. Total Paid and/or Requested Circulation (sum of 15b(1) and 15b(2))	46,289	47,741
d. Free Distribution by Mail, Samples, Complimentary, and Other Free	200	200
e. Free Distribution Outside the Mail		
f. Total Distribution (sum of 15d and 15e)	200	200
g. Total Distribution (sum of 15c and 15f)	46,489	47,941
h. Copies Not Distributed		
1. Office Use, Leftovers, Spoiled	6,301	3,537
2. Returns from News Agents		
i. Total (sum of 15g, 15h(1), and 15h(2))	52,790	51,478
Percent Paid and/or Requested Circulation (15c/15g × 100)	100	100

16. This Statement of Ownership will be printed in the 2003, vol. 1, no. 1 issue of this publication.
17. I certify that all information furnished on this form is true and complete. I understand that anyone who furnishes false or misleading information on this form or who omits material or information requested on the form may be subject to criminal sanctions (including fines and imprisonment) and/or civil sanctions (including multiple damages and civil penalties).

Signature and Title of Editor, Publisher, Business Manager, or Owner
Jaynee Dudley, Publisher